From Arys to Harwi

from War -Torn Europe to Post- War England

Paul aged twelve.

Richard J Ellison

This book is dedicated to those thousands of German refugees who lost their lives both in escaping from East Prussia ahead of the advancing Russian army during the winter of 1944/1945 and subsequently in the refugee camps in Denmark during the 1940s.

Contents

Acknowledgements

In writing a book which involves a lot of personal testimony and including information from many sources, I have relied on a number of people who have been so very helpful and kind and have freely given of their time. This is gratefully acknowledged and very much appreciated. Without this invaluable assistance this book could not be written and this amazing story would not have been told.

Of course, it goes without saying that without Paul there would be no book. Knowing what I now know particularly of the trek through East Prussia and the post war period in Denmark, it is miraculous that he and his mother Lydia did survive. Basically this is his story and his testimony set in a context of the 1930s and 1940s. I have simply crafted what he has told me into a book by taking notes during our very interesting chats, over a cup of tea and scones or piece of cake. I have also added varying amounts of historical context to give some background. At time Paul's memories have brought on a few tears and I often gained a metaphorical lump in my throat.

I hope I have done the story justice. I have had great fun in tracking down the information and in travelling to both Denmark and Poland. The good old internet has been invaluable. Those that read the book will have to make up their own minds.
The reader will note that sometimes I have recalled past conversations that took place on the trek or in Denmark in German or English. This is how Paul has remembered what happened all those years ago.

I am also really grateful for the assistance of the former National Children's Home, now Action for Children, in particular Helen Lavelle, the Engagement Manager in the London Watford Office of Action for Children whose help has been fantastic. She was able to track down old NCH files for me to inspect at the Watford office and these gave me a real insight into how the brilliant scheme for the transfer of German children to England, after the 1939-1945 war, was set up.

The same charity was able to give Paul his NCH personal file which has also revealed valuable information as you will see as the story unfolds.
A contact I made following my trip to Poland in May June 2019, via email, Dietrich Peylo has been brilliant. He who also, like the Ciekas (pronounced Seeka), escaped Arys in the winter of 1944/45, with his family, boarding the last train to leave the town in January 1945. He has provided invaluable help and information about Arys in the 1930s and 1940s. I am really indebted to him for his assistance and also for his kind gift of a book of old postcards of Arys and the surrounding area; various elements of which he has allowed me to reproduce in my book. He has also provided a historical link to the town for which I am very grateful. His family also lived in Arys from October 1936 and he was born on 14th January 1936, just before Paul in February 1936. What another amazing link to the past! I am so fortunate to have found him.

Whilst on the subject of my visit to Poland, I must also record my appreciation of the help given to me by the curator of the local museum, Katarzyna Galczak-Slezak and her assistant Lukasz Wolski. A great deal of information was provided; permission was given to incorporate some postcards into the book and copies of maps provided. With their kind assistance, our visit to Orzysz would not have been so successful and I would never have contacted Dietrich.

For the Danish research, Bill Young, a close friend and also, like Paul, a member of St. Andrews church, was very kind in putting me in touch with his son Niall Young who is married to a Danish lady and lives in Denmark. Niall was brilliant in helping me to gain access to information from the

Danish National Archives in Copenhagen about Danish refugee camps in the 1940s. He also managed, with some backing from me and support from one of my Danish contacts, to persuade the museum at Viborg that they really did have some information about the Ciekas despite previously being adamant that they held no information on German refugees. My trip to Copenhagen is described in a very light-hearted way in a later chapter of this book.

Despite what I have written in that chapter, during my trip, I did receive very helpful assistance from a number of people in the National Archives in Copenhagen and I must mention Karen Jensen in particular, at the Immigration Museum in Farum, who gave me a number of very useful Danish contacts.

These have all been extremely valuable in helping me to gain a more thorough understanding of that period in Danish history. But in particular I must mention a number of individuals.

Leif Hansen Neilsen has been so helpful in that he has provided most useful descriptions of the refugee camps in the Sonderborg area of Denmark.

I have also incorporated relevant extracts from other books written by a number of authors on the subject in good faith that these are an accurate portrayal of the period.

Henrik Havrehed notes, in his book about German refugees in the period 1945-1949, that in the Danish Census of 1946, 196, 518 German refugees resided in Denmark. His view is that, despite these numbers, these refugees "have so far received little attention in historical and genealogical research. "This has prompted him to set up a database for German refugees in Denmark

Martin Reimers, who has been doing research on German military camps in Denmark, has also helped me with regard to the source of certain documents regarding Horupt Klint camp and published information about German refugees and life in the camps.

To all these very helpful and friendly people I say a really big thank you for giving up time to assist me in my research.

It is hoped this book can contribute perhaps, in some small way, to telling the story of one family's personal journey.

Author's Note

Please note that I have tried to use the names of places as they were at the time of Paul's story together with their modern day equivalent if it is different, for example Arys later became Orzysz.

Sometimes, for example, in the case of the former East Prussia area or part of it, now in Poland, I have used the modern day equivalent only if I don't know the war time name.

My intention has been to assist the reader should he or she wish to locate these names on old or new maps of Europe and so try to trace the route followed by Paul and his mum. There is a map later in the book which aims to give the reader some help in following the route taken by Paul and Lydia Cieka.

Other Books by the Same Author

Accidents, Incidents and Adventures in the Atlas Mountains of Morocco.

Introduction

I have known Paul Cieka for a number of years as a Methodist minister, attached in one way or another to St. Andrews Methodist Church in Winsford in the heart of rural Cheshire.

More recently, Paul has retired from the Ministry and he has become a valued friend to me and to my wife Sue. He has also been very positive and supportive to me personally in my efforts to take on a more active role, as a Church steward, in the life of St. Andrews Methodist church.

In getting to know Paul I have also become aware that Paul has had a very colourful personal history in more ways than one. Little did I know though, of the extent of the story of his own childhood first in Germany, then in Denmark and finally in the UK. This was both traumatic and equally amazing and I now know why Paul himself feels indebted to and is so supportive of the National Children's Home (NCH), now the charity Action for Children, for the majority of his life.

As I have said Paul has been a long standing and influential Methodist minister for more years than he would care to remember.

I will always remember with fondness and emotion, the first time I heard him preach when he said in his opening address " It is both an honour and privilege for me to preach to you today at St. Andrews." I will always remember those words.

I realised that this very humble man was certainly worth listening to and that his own style of preaching, always appreciative of the opportunity to talk to and lead the congregation in worship, for that is what he did, owed a great deal to his own personal life journey and his experiences gained along the way.

This view has certainly been reinforced through my reading of Paul's personal records from the time of his early life in the National Children's Home. He has only recently obtained this bulging file and suffice to say it has brought back many memories and reminders of those early years in the UK and certainly one or two tears as well. From that file, he has found out many things that he didn't know or possibly had forgotten with the passage of time.

It has been my good fortune also, in more recent years, to be present when Paul has preached from the pulpit at St. Andrew's church, particularly at services for Action for Children, formerly the NCH.

It was at such services that Paul talked with great emotion of his childhood in Germany before and during the Second World War, under Hitler's Third Reich. I became very interested in and was certainly touched by his story. Pleased with my interest, Paul gratefully sent me the occasional letter with a bit more detail of his life in 1930s and 1940s Germany. It was fascinating and I was intrigued to learn more particularly because I had completed a project on the 'Rise and Fall of the Third Reich' whilst at Secondary school.

As time passed and I heard the same compelling story on a few further occasions at church services and, as our friendship developed, I took the opportunity to encourage Paul to write down his memories, perhaps in a diary or book. This is a story that must be told for the benefit of existing and future generations, I thought to myself.

Whether the task seemed too onerous for him to take on in later years or the memories were too difficult to recall or there was a worry about what the past would evoke, Paul seemed to side step the whole issue. Ah, well, I thought it must be too daunting for him, the memories too painful, and I decided not to pursue the matter further. Little did I know that Paul had already tried to write down his memories of his family life in 1930s/1940s Germany and in Denmark. He had even been interviewed by Action for Children about this time in his life but for whatever reason he had not persevered to complete his own story.

Paul, however, has over the years, continued to be very supportive of Action for Children. As recently as 2015 he took part in a joint service which was dedicated to this charity, at St. Andrew' Methodist church in Winsford, Cheshire

Once again he reminisced about the Second World War and his journey with his mother, as refugees travelling from the town of Arys in East Prussia, Germany to Denmark, through war-torn Europe in that very harsh winter of 1944/45.

I was very moved again and I suspect so were many others in the congregation. Paul appeared to be quite emotional as he recalled the events of some 70 years ago. But once again I thought to myself this is an amazing story that must be told.

I decided to give it 'one last shot' perhaps not the most appropriate phrase for such a story. But I was determined to see if I could persuade Paul this time to complete the story of his memories. However, this time I decided to adopt a different approach.

Paul is from the old school and this is no criticism. He still likes to write letters in a wonderfully flowery script, amazing in these times of text and e-mail.

Such letters from Paul, when I get them, are a joy to receive. I look forward to them, so I thought perhaps that could be the answer. I will do the same. I will write to him or rather send him a typed letter as my handwriting is not that wonderful.

So this is what I did. Without going into too much detail, in my letter, I basically encouraged Paul to tell his story to me through weekly personal meetings. I would take notes, ask him questions and just let him talk. I decided that using a tape recorder would be too intrusive and much too formal.

He obviously thought about my suggestion for some time, but eventually to quote the vernacular, he said in another of his wonderful letters that he was "gob smacked" at my suggestion and wanted "to give it a go." I was really pleased particularly as I was about to end my career in Town Planning

Consultancy and wanted to have a go at writing a book. Here was a heaven sent opportunity with so much interesting material to hand.

Conscious of the sensitivity of the subject matter, I re-assured Paul that I was sure he would be happy with the contents of the book; after all it was his story.

It was therefore agreed that we would have our first meeting/discussion and see how matters progressed. It was clear that some historical context would be necessary for this traumatic period of world history and that we both would have homework to do. The internet was a great source of information and I was able to provide Paul with source material which I hoped we could use to prompt his memory. After all we were talking about a time many, many years ago. This has proved to be a very successful way of reaching back into Paul's memory.

I have read a number of personal testimonies from people who have served in the armed forces during the Second World War as adults and what strikes me most is that their memory of such times is so good. Perhaps we do remember more in our later years of what happened a long time ago.

What is remarkable about Paul's story is that it is from his childhood. How many of us can recall all the detail from our childhood and we have more to go on such as letters, school reports, photographs and postcards? Paul has none of these, as many of the family records were lost on the trek and yet he still has some remarkable details of certain incidents, from his memory.

As I complete the book I can confirm that, Paul and I did meet many times. We secured his NCH records and Action for Children encouraged me to visit their office in Watford, Hertfordshire to search their archives. That task has been completed and new information has come to light regarding the background to the movement of children from central Europe to the UK.

Whilst on the subject of the NCH, I am extremely pleased to report that Dietrich Peylo, has a view on the good work done by the charity in the 1940s –"I greatly appreciate the Methodist N C H, that helped German kids by real human attitude." It is so nice to have a German national supporting the work of the charity.

We have enlisted the help of Hans Peter, Paul's brother, who lives in Germany. He has provided us with some German records and a photograph of the boys' father smartly dressed in his German Wehrmacht uniform. I can confirm that there is more to report concerning Paul's dad in a later chapter of this book

The impact of researching for this book, talking to Paul and actually typing the text on my lap top and visiting both Denmark and Poland has had a significant impact on me. Whilst Paul has unfortunately re-visited in his dreams some of the incidents which took place on his journey to Denmark, the effect on me has been more subtle.

Whilst compiling this story I have developed a deeply held respect for all those refugees who have trekked across Europe to escape from both the Nazis and the Russians.

All the suffering has made me realise how very fortunate my generation is not to have experienced the impact of war which my parent's had to go through. But at the same time I am convinced of the necessity and importance of telling Paul's story so that others, the readers of this book, may know of and understand the suffering experienced by children, their mothers and elderly people, many of whom who didn't survive this particular journey, in the war-torn Europe of the 1940s. Hopefully future generations will do their best to prevent such calamities.

I feel privileged to have been given the opportunity to record what was certainly an unforgettable journey and what makes the story all the more remarkable is that every time Paul and I have met he is reliving those events. Amazing!

I hope that Paul will agree that I have accurately portrayed his story, and that I have done it justice.

Richard Ellison   Summer 2019

Chapter 1

A Friendly Invasion

This seems to be a contradiction in terms. But it is the title given to the planned movement of a number of German children, made refugees as a result of World War II, to England in the late 1940s. This was made possible by the forethought, good organisation and compassion of the charity the NCH, in the post war period.

Some people could have seen these young ones, including Paul, arriving in England, as the children of the former enemy and indeed a photograph taken of Paul in 1948, on the cover of this book, shows a young blond German. Surely his appearance would have made him a strong candidate for the Hitler Youth? Fortunately these victims of war were made very welcome in the UK. Clearly we know that Paul arrived safe and sound in the port of Harwich otherwise he and I would never have met and become friends and this book would never have been written.

But how did all this happen? I was very curious and wanted to try to find out the background if I could.

The Second World War was characterised by a number of amazing humanitarian gestures and rescue stories: the well-known Oscar Schindler Jewish story which spawned a great film. There was also the less well known Raol Wallenberg and Pinchas Tibor Rosenbaum, two men who endangered their lives for months on end and managed to save hundreds of Jews, individuals and families, during the darkest days of the Second World War in

Budapest, Hungary and also there was Sir Nicholas Winton in Czechoslovakia and Austria.

But our story is different!

However, before the story of Paul's journey from Arys to Harwich is told, I will try to give some explanation as to the background to Paul's migration from Denmark to the UK and the role of the NCH and others in the successful transfer of children from war-torn Europe to the relative stability of the UK.

My extensive examination of the former NCH files, held at their HQ in Watford, Hertfordshire, reveals that 118 children were admitted into the UK in 1948 under what was known as the UK's Hospitality scheme.

The origin of schemes such as this stemmed from the 'Riversmead Scheme' which was set up by the Christian Council for the Care of Refugees from Germany and Central Europe in collaboration with the NCH and the Social Welfare Department of the Methodist Church. The aim was to provide a safe haven for young male German and Austrian Christians who were in danger from the policies of Hitler because of their Jewish ancestry.

The Riversmead house was closed in 1942 and, following its success, the Hospitality Scheme was introduced in 1946. This was set up by NCH and the aim was to provide a home for about 100 children who were currently living in refugee camps on the continent. In total over 120 children were brought over, 86 boys and 34 girls.

The impetus for these arrangements was a bit of a mystery to me. However it all became clear when I came across a letter dated 2nd December 1947 from Jens Bloomer, the Head of the Danish Refugee Administration based in Copenhagen, addressed to Mrs Gertrude Evans of the World Council of Churches in London.

This letter in fact refers to an earlier letter of 21st May 1947 by the Rev. Henry Carter to the Rev. Halfdan Hogsbro of the Church Service for Refugees in Denmark, a copy of which must have gone to the Danish Refugee Administration. This explains that the NCH " has offered to receive a number of orphans of the age group 9-12 selected from among the German refugees staying in Denmark at the present time, it being the intention that these children shall be educated and stay in the said Home for a period of 5 or 6 years."

The reply on 25th August 1947 from Rev. Hafdan Hogsbro to the Rev. Henry Carter was very positive and included a list of seven orphaned boys. The letter also asked whether the NCH and Orphanage would wish to receive a number of non-orphans of the same age, provided the parents agreed to the children, during the said period, receiving education and training on the same conditions as the orphans.

It was just as well that non-orphans were allowed to come to the UK for without this additional category of refugee children being selected Paul would never have made it to the UK.

On 14th October 1947, Mrs G Evans, in a letter, asked the Rev. Hogsbro to try to find some more children, for instance a number of 20, and transmit a list of names, with the consent of their parents, to a Mr Rees in Geneva. (I am not sure of his role in this proposed movement of refugee children).

All this does sound very bureaucratic but I suppose it was necessary because of the sensitivity of allowing German refugee children to come to the UK and I am sure the authorities and the NCH would have wanted the transfer to run as smoothly as possible.

Unfortunately, this was not the end of the red tape. The next task for the hard working Rev. Hogsbro, clearly a significant player in all these arrangements, was to request the Danish Refugee Administration to select from the many German refugee camps a number of children likely to benefit from both training and education in the NCH and Orphanage.

Jens Blosmer duly sent Mrs Evans a list of 29 children, at present in German refugee camps, of ages 9-13, of which 6 were orphans. He also confirmed that for the other 23 children, copies of parental declarations agreeing to their children going to England for the said period of 6 years, plus a medical certificate as to their state of health would also be sent. I have in fact seen these documents for Paul.

A copy of the original letter, from Paul's dad, plus Paul's translation, for my benefit, is included in the next few pages.

Jens Blosmer also added that "as soon we have been informed that the said children will be granted immigration permits to England, we shall see to it that the children be provided with passports for aliens with exit visas, adding that the passports do not entitle the children to go to Denmark again." Clearly the Danish Authorities didn't want these children back again!

The photograph shown on the next page is a photocopy of the original certificate which gives permission by the Danish Authorities for 25 refugee children including Paul Cieka, number 14, to leave Denmark. It also confirms that these German children have been in Denmark as refugees.

It has also been stamped at the British Embassy in Copenhagen and therefore comprises a group visa for the 25 children to travel to England.

The original document is in remarkably good condition given its age, all thanks to being kept in an old NCH file which mercifully had been not thrown away.

With all the necessary documents and permissions in place, 'The Friendly Invasion' could now begin.

Sunday morning January 11th 1948 saw a group of 25 children, the first to arrive at Harwich, from a defeated and suffering Germany. They had been gathered at Hanover by the kindly cooperation of the Friends Relief Service and had journeyed for twenty four hours over land and sea.

Their arrival represented the first visible result of months of planning and preparation by a number of organisations both in England and on main land Europe.

They were the forerunners of a total number of 118 including our Paul, received into the NCH from overseas during January to July 1948, under a scheme approved by the Home Office of the UK government. The terms were:

"It is understood that the proposal is to select promising children, both girls and boys who are likely to profit by an education in England and to return eventually to Germany or Austria, where it is hoped, they will help in the re-education of their countrymen. The children will all be young, generally under twelve, though there may be a few not older than fourteen. (The age range for those in Paul's group of 25 was from 9-14 years of age.)

They will be selected after a medical examination, which will take account both of their physical health and of their mental ability. (We are not sure how this second factor was tested although on Paul's NCH registration document it states that he has attained an education standard of 7 year and that the stage reached for his education is Elementary.)

The National Children's Home will be responsible for their maintenance and care during their stay in England and for their return home when their time comes to an end. Whilst the Home Secretary relies on the promoters of the scheme to select the children, and to organise their training with a view to the eventual return of most of them to their home countries, he recognises that it may be found later that there are exceptional grounds for allowing some of them to remain in this country, and sympathetic consideration will be given to any such requests."

We must remember that the language used by the Home Secretary is reflective of the times and the action taken was in response to a particular urgent difficulty concerning the future of particularly German refugees in Denmark where there was no immediate prospect of repatriation to post war Germany whose economy lay in ruins, where there was a real shortage of food and good quality housing and a stable family life was not always possible.

Paul is number 14. And this is his Visa to travel to the UK. I wonder how many of these became very good friends of Paul and how many of them went to the home that he first went to. How many of them could we contact after the book is published.

On page 22 is the permission from Paul's father for him to go to England with the benefit of the English translation underneath.

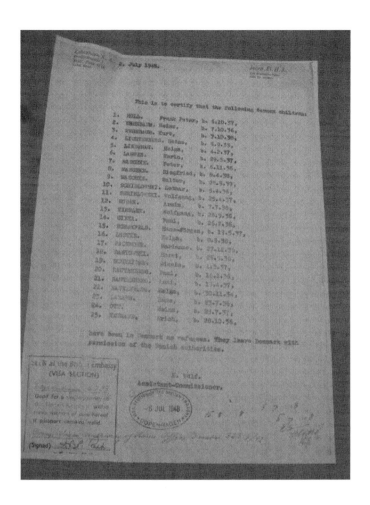

This is a list of children travelling to the UK which includes Paul.

It was provided courtesy of Action For Children and came from an old NCH file held at their offices in Watford, Herts.

On 5th March, a second party, some 29 children, 25 boys and 4 girls, ages ranging from 9 to 14, came from Displaced Persons Camps in Denmark. These were children, like Paul, but Paul came later, who had fled before the advancing Russians at the end of the war, most from East Prussia and had been hurriedly shipped to Denmark. Some like Paul were with their mothers and had been forced to live behind barbed wire since crossing into Denmark with food according to the NCH, "provided by the International Red Cross and not by the Danes themselves," but others were orphans as their mothers had either not survived the journey or the conditions in the camps.

It appears that the food was exactly calculated with scientific precision to keep them healthy but "was utterly monotonous," confirmed the NCH. It was noted that "two of the parties of children which came from Danish camps went into raptures over breakfast eggs given to them on arrival here. In the camps, eggs had to be reserved for TB sufferers."

They had been in the camps for three years, before coming to England.

But according to the NCH," the Danish government will not maintain the camps and the occupants must be dispersed."

Although the NCH were taking the children, many of which were orphans because their mothers hadn't survived the journey, "such parents as remain are being moved back to Germany where they will have to re-establish themselves in very difficult conditions." This indeed was the fate of Lydia Cieka and Paul's brother Hans Peter.

The NCH also were being urged to take more refugees- "we have been begged by the Danish escorts, who accompanied the children, to take a further group if at all possible."

The pressure to take more children continued, as one of the escorts put it, "to us in Denmark where there are still 44,000 Displaced Persons in the camps, twenty nine seems such a little number. But to the children it means everything."

Following this second group of children, came a third party on 30th April, some twenty six from Germany itself and finally on 8th July the last party arrived, twenty five more children from the Danish Camps. It was this third group which was to contain Paul! Without his inclusion in this group there would have been no story.

Interestingly, it is the final party, which contained Paul, about whom we have some more information.

There were more boys than girls, comprising 20 families in total. Of their mothers, five were dead, nineteen still in Displaced Persons Camps (including Lydia Cieka), and of one there was no information. Further, with regard to the whereabouts of their fathers, thirteen were killed in the war, nine others were missing and so presumed dead, one was in a Danish

Displaced Persons Camp and two were still working, one as a Farm Inspector, this was Paul's dad, Paul Senior and one was a bank clerk. It is noted by the NCH that "the wife and child of each," (one family is Lydia and Hans Peter) "were in a Displaced Persons Camp."

It is amazing that we can actually pin point at this time where all the Ciekas were living! Father Paul was living in Eutin, Holstein. But the reunion of the parents was at that time prevented by the combined Military Zonal Authorities.

It is my hope, that the writing of this book, might possibly result in contact being made, perhaps via the charity 'Action For Children' with those children, now adults, who were on the same list as Paul. Possibly, a second Edition of the book could be produced!

For the first few weeks the children were based at a Sunshine House, and were referred to as the 'Sunshine children' at Alverstoke. Afterwards, the children were dispersed to different branches of the NCH. The vast majority of children had returned to Germany by 1951, once their relatives had been located, but some did remain on in the UK, Paul was one of them!

Chapter 2

Family Background and Early Life in East Prussia

So we now know more of the background as to how it was that Paul came to be allowed to leave Denmark to go to the UK but before we find out about his dramatic departure from his home town of Arys in 1944, we need to explore his early life in Germany. So we now come to that part of the story.

Paul Robert Johannes Cieka was born on February 26th, 1936 in the Germany Army Garrison camp of Arys (now Orzysz), a small town in East Prussia, now located in Poland. This was in the district of Kreis Johannisburg. He was the first child of parents Paul Robert Johannes Cieka and Lydia Auguste Elisabeth Cieka, (nee Schroder). Paul tells me that there were in fact two midwives at his birth which was a 'home confinement.' This probably occurred in the family flat on the army base. Probably Paul senior had been transferred there as Germany expanded its army and its bases..

There is some evidence to suggest that, in 1930s Germany, the authorities decided that many "midwives were a way to get into the homes and make sure they were proper Aryan homes." (Lynne Fallwell, 'Modern German Midwifery, 1885–1960.') It seems that the idea was that midwives could go into homes and make an assessment on behalf of the party. With Paul's father in the Wehrmacht presumably there was no problem. When the Nazis seized power in 1933, midwives officially became part of the national health system.

But it appears that Nazism also favoured midwives and home births as a cost-saving measure. The reasoning was that the less that had to be spent on maternity costs, after all, the more that could be spent on the preparations for war.

I suspect Paul was named after his father and grandfather which may have been a prevailing tradition at the time of his birth. What we do know is that the name Paul was not particularly popular among Germans in 1930s, it being the 34th most popular boy's name, according to the Internet.

His home, whilst within the Army garrison camp, it was really part of the town as well.

Now I know from our discussions that his memory of 1930s and1940s Germany is quite remarkable. It is truly amazing what he has revealed to me each time we have met but I don't believe for one moment that he remembers the particular event of his birth! I am sure his mother told him all about it.

It appears that in 1930s Germany, there was no birth certificates like those we have in the UK, but there is a German document, a Certificate of Nationality (see below) which seems to confirm Paul's date of birth as correct. This was needed to establish Paul's identity as all the family papers were lost after they fled Arys and to prove who he was. His parents also had to produce a 'Statement under Oath' to confirm their identity with all their personal details. This must have all been very stressful.

It is likely that Paul's birth was not registered in the same way as births are registered today. Rather mum, Lydia Cieka, would have made a sworn statement to the local Commissioner of Oaths in Arys, giving details of the birth plus the names and backgrounds of mother and father. Paul's father would have presented his army identity card as evidence of his credentials.

Paul's parents were both born in East Prussia, in the early Twentieth Century, father Paul at Wehlau on 9 February 1908, a town with many German Lutherans. Until World War II the town of Wehlau was known mostly for its horse markets. Mother Lydia was born at Stalluponen on 30 November 1910. It became Ebenrode in1938 as its previous name sounded to un-German for the Nazis.

Paul's parents were married in Ebenrode, following the tradition of marriage in the bride's town, on 9th February 1935.

I am sure that both parents were very excited at the prospect of the birth of their first child brought into the world to live in the upstairs apartment of the married quarters for Wehrmacht officers. Paul's Dad, Ober Lieutenant Cieka, was a young officer who served in the Pay Corps of the army garrison.

Both parents were convinced that the baby would be a girl. It is unknown as to why they had reached that conclusion without the aid of a modern scan, perhaps it was the shape or position of the bump. Grandparents will often look at the expectant mother and give their view. Nevertheless, their hopes and excitement were shared by all the family and so many gifts for a baby girl arrived.

But it was on 26 February 1936 that baby Paul arrived in their apartment. It was rumoured that he spent the first 3 to 7 weeks dressed in pink! Paul confirms that the content of this tale depends on which of the four Schroder uncles, Paul, Peter, Arnold or Erich is doing the telling.

Presumably there was no opportunity to return the pink clothes and replace them with blue as there was no German equivalent of the shop 'Mothercare' in existence at that time.

The registration of the birth was left almost to the last day when father showed his army pay book and Paul received the same names as his father.

Paul has described to me that his early life took its natural course, difficult to believe in 1930s Germany under Adolf Hitler. He was baptised in the Evangelische (Protestant) church in Arys and from the age of four, in 1940, started to attend Kindegarten, where he was introduced to P.E. for the first time. He also attended the church Sunday school until he fled Arys with his mother in December 1944.

I have tracked down, courtesy of the internet, some old postcards of Arys to see what Paul remembers about his birth place. He recalls some shops and the white market building and the white church with its spire and cross. These are included in this book in a later chapter which describes my visit to the town of Paul's birth.

He was later to excel at running on arrival in the UK but I am 'jumping the gun', (another unfortunate metaphor) here and I am getting ahead of myself.

He recalls that his early life was full of interest and discovery, largely because he was living in a military garrison camp. Arys was known as a military town. I bet it was very exciting with all those soldiers doing drills and on parade and all the army equipment and machines including tanks.

He remembers that during the war, from 1939, all the gates and entrances to the camp were heavily guarded, both day and night. It is helpful here to add some additional information about the camp, particularly its history as far as I have been able to find out.

During the First World War, the Military Training Ground at Arys was in the Russian Tsar's hands. The occupation lasted from August 21st to September 8th 1914 and from 10 November 1914 to February 12, 1915. Soldiers who were killed or died in a field hospital were mostly from Germany, Russia, and England or from the French army. They were buried next to each other in the suburban cemetery.

A new era began for the town in the 1930s with the ascension of the Fascists in Europe. In 1934, the Nazis started to modernise the barracks at the edge of the town and the surrounding area was revived. Soldiers of different formations trained on the second largest training camp in Germany.

Up until 1937, the military training grounds at Arys were being expanded up to 20,000 hectares (ha) from 4416 ha. Between 1921 and 1926, the training grounds were used to test artillery and rifle weapons and as result a system of bunkers, used during the manoeuvres, was built. From old photographs we know that there was a firing range at Arys too. From 1934–1937, the training grounds were expanded by adding the villages of Szwejkowo and Oszczylwiki whose inhabitants were relocated. Some 4256 ha of forest land was also included. A barrack camp in Wierzbiny and summer barracks in Bemowo Piskie were also increased in size.

It seems as if the re-introduction of general compulsory military service in June 1935 in Germany may well have had something to do with the expansion of the Army training area. In 1939, the training grounds received the name of Obóz Ćwiczebny Orzysz (Training Camp Orzysz) and Wehrmacht troops were quartered here

On this page is an aerial photograph of Arys with the camp on the right side of the picture, Paul's church towards the top of the picture next to a double gable white building and the Kommandant's house can be clearly seen surrounded by trees, middle right.

The disproportionate separation of the province of East Prussia, post 1918, from the rest of the German Reich through the corridor of the Memel area actually made many of its inhabitants, believe it or not, trust the National Socialists (Nazis).There was also hope for a revision of the Versailles Treaty which ended World War I and which had disastrous repercussions for Germany. But the Second World War actually led to even greater catastrophe as we know from history.

Largely spared by the war until the middle of January 1945, the town of Arys witnessed a dreary calm. It was the propaganda, threats and the failure of the German Reich and those responsible, which prevented a legitimate evacuation of the civilian population.

At the same time, in addition to the main camp at Arys, another troop camp, some 12 kms south of Arys, was built at Schlagakrug in the parish of Drygallen/Drigelsdorf. This was called Arys Sud, with the main camp now known as Arys Nord.

Arys - Sud had a very different appearance to its larger counterpart and was laid out in a very modern way in the forest with a large sports swimming pool at its centre. At the end of the 1930s it was able to accommodate a regiment and also two divisions. In the 1940s, the camp was mainly used by army troops. Shortly before the Second World War a bunker was built to train the troops for battle against a modern army in an advanced position.

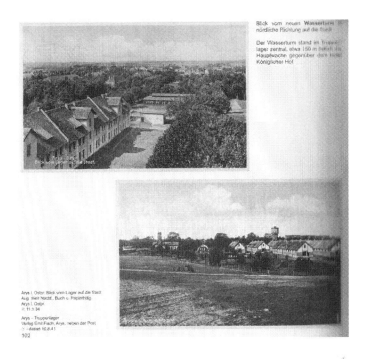

These are two more postcards of the main camp, one from the water tower, dated 1934 looking north to Arys and the other looking towards it, dated 1941, both courtesy of Dietrich Peylo.

Troops from Arys participated in the invasion of Poland and fought in the battle of Wizna.

The Battle of Wizna was fought between September 7 and September 10, 1939, between the forces of Poland and Germany during the initial stages of invasion of Poland

During WWII, military units were trained on the training grounds in Orzysz before being sent to the front. General Rommel, the "Desert Fox" exercised his tanks there before the African campaign. In addition, many new weapons were tested under the guidance of the highest dignitaries of the third German Reich. (Source: Orzysz website).

Please note that some of the names I have used may be the names used today i.e. Polish names, for example Orzysz was Arys.

In the spring of 1939, one of the soldiers wrote from Arys to a family in Bochum, "we have seen in the East Prussia sands, pine forests and endless roads and lakes. The sun burns our brains. After 15 kilometres of march we can barely stand on our feet. Sleepless nights are had for our physical condition. The camp is kept in the best order."

On this page is a postcard of the Army Camp in Arys.

On this page is a postcard of Arys in 1935 of soldiers marching through the town.

A young boy recalls at the time, "Often I stood in the balcony of the hotel and watched as the soldiers passed by with music playing. In our small town usually there were many spectators- watching. But then there were the long silent columns at the Hotel Konglicher Hof in the station street. The trains for the troop transport going to the East were already waiting at the station. For many who had spent days in front of the photo studio in our yard, it became a journey without return."

The source for this quote is Dietrich Peylo's book of postcards of Arys as it is for the two postcards which appear on the next page.

The top postcard is four views of Arys Troop Camp: the war memorial possibly from the WW1, the officer's Kasino or restaurant/mess facilities, troops entering one of the main gates and the main guard room. The bottom postcard is of soldiers' accommodation.

It seems also that new tanks were tried out at Arys. On August 5th, 1943, it was decided to mount a modified Tiger I heavy tank with a 380mm rocket launcher/mortar installed in a new superstructure. The new vehicle received the designation of 38cm RW61 auf Sturm(panzer) morser Tiger, but it was also known as Sturmtiger, Sturmpanzer VI and

Tiger-Morser. The most common designation used was Sturmtiger-Assault Tiger.

Nach Kriegsende 1918 wurde der Truppenübungsplatz Arys zunächst stillgelegt. 1920/21 während des polnisch-russischen Krieges waren bis zu 45.000 russische Militärpersonen auf dem Lagergelände interniert. Während der Reichswehrzeit gab es nur einen sehr eingeschränkten Übungsbetrieb. Das brachte auch einen wirtschaftlichen Niedergang für die Stadt Arys mit sich. In den 30er-Jahren wurde das Truppenlager in Arys modernisiert, nun **Arys-Nord** genannt.

pen-Übungslager Arys – Nord
Nwache – Offiziers-Kasino –
erdenkmal
g. Julius Welt, Papierhdlg., Arys, O.-Pr.
7.39

. Ostpr. – Truppen-Übungslager
nd Peylo, gegenüber der Hauptwache,
. Ostpr.
10.39 Feldpost

On October 20th, 1943, the first prototype Sturmtiger was presented to Adolf Hitler at the training facilities at Arys (Orzysz) in East Prussia. This prototype was based on a mid-production Tiger I (rubber road wheels) and had the superstructure made of iron armour plates (soft steel). It was extensively tested and, in April 1944, production was approved.

Having shown Paul an old photograph of Hitler inspecting tanks, he announced nonchalantly: "oh yes I remember standing on a mound overlooking the airfield with other children waving flags when Uncle Adolf's aeroplane touched down." Amazing, I thought to recall such a moment of history and to have actually been present when Adolf Hitler arrived to inspect a new tank! More details of the Roski airfield can be found in the later chapter, 'Return to Arys' I have seen photographs of the tank with Hitler inspecting but unfortunately I have not been able to obtain permission to put either in my book found below. A search of Pinterest for Sturmtiger prototype during presentation on front of Hitler on Arys proving grounds, October 1943 will provide the photos.

Along with the military investments, a tourist infrastructure developed very dynamically in Orzysz with rapid development in the 20's and 30's of the 20th

century. Youth tourism was significant after Hitler had come to power in 1933, with tourism and sport an important part of the Nazi ideology.

In terms of the accommodation and catering facilities in Orzysz on the premises of the military holiday centre the so-called Dworzec Gościnny (Guest House) "Budda" was established. There was a large restaurant, hotel and bathing beach. In summer, an army band played and in winter, an ice rink was prepared. Near the guest house there was a villa of the hunting association. There were also small hotels in Orzysz in the inter war period: Deutsches Haus, Hohenzollern - with a cafe of the same name, Kaiserhof, Koeniglicher Hof, and Treiber (a total of 5 hotels). Aside from the hotels, a youth hostel, offering free accommodation and breakfasts to students, was established in Orzysz. As for catering facilities, there were 6 restaurants, 1 cafe, 2 beer bars and 1 wine bar. Orzysz was a local railway node and 6 trains a day ran from Pisz (Johannisburg) to Orzysz and Giżycko. Before the outbreak of WWII in 1939 the town had a population of 3,543. (All these details have been obtained from the Orzysz web site).

Perhaps this explains part of the reason why there are so many old postcards of Arys in existence. Soldiers would often write home about the numerous shops all competing against each other. The postcards document the townscape, the recreational facilities

Living on the military camp, we know that Paul lived with his parents in a flat, which was in a two storey building, approximately fifty to one hundred metres long, with a good level of accommodation as befits an officer in the German army. Ober-Lieutenant Cieka, in the Wehrmacht, and his small family had the use of 2 bedrooms, a kitchen, bathroom, toilet and living room. As an officer also, Cieka senior received special food provisions, although we have no details of these goodies.

This was because the camp kitchens, where food was cooked daily, were below the Cieka's flat and the family received officer fringe benefits. On the ground floor also was a very large dining room plus single officer quarters and storage space.

Paul recalls that when his father was present he didn't talk much about the war. I expect many children whose parents fought in the war can recall a similar experience. I know that with my own situation that I really only found out what my dad did in the Second World War when I acquired his RAF service record recently. It was really fascinating and I do very much regret not talking to my dad about his time in the RAF.

Paul does remember however, that his dad's army friends did visit for meals and there was the smoking of cigars and there was a great deal of singing. There was also lots of German beer. A popular song was 'Ich hatt einen Kameraden':

> "I once had a Comrade,
>
> You will find no better.
>
> The drum called to battle,
>
> He walked at my side,
>
> In the same pace and step."

There were a lot of variations and Paul recalls "he was one of the best, a very good man and you won't find a better one." The song is a traditional lament of the German Armed Forces.

Also known as 'The Good Comrade,' it is still plays an important ceremonial role in the German Armed Forces and is an integral part of a military funeral, continuing a tradition started at some point around 1871. Another connection with Arys is that the song was also played at Erwin *Johannes* (one of Paul's names) Eugen Rommel's funeral which took place in Ulm, Germany on 18th October 1944.

Paul says of his dad that generally he wore his uniform most of the time and that he was a very proud man. I suspect Dad would have also been very proud of his wife and son trekking across Germany to a sort of freedom in Denmark.

Thinking back, Paul can clearly picture the camp with an Officers' Restaurant and Assembly Hall and rooms. Between 1940 and 1943, officers' children celebrated Christmas at a party in the big hall. Paul cannot forget also the splendid, large house which was the Commandant's residence with its heavily guarded access. Old postcards of the camp provide strong confirmation of Paul's recollections.

Life in a military camp however did have its hardships, the brick barracks were very cold in the long winters of East Prussia, with the bitter east winds coming straight from the Urals. There were large stoves taking wood and coal which provided some much needed heat for the Cieka flat.

The area surrounding the military camp comprised the town of Arys which itself was part of an area known as the Masuren Lakes Plateau. There were often trips to go fishing in the Lake Aryssee.

Just off shore there was an island. In the shallow waters between the edge of the lake and the island in summer Lydia taught Paul to swim breast stroke. Mother was obviously very conscious of the fact that boys will be boys and inevitably lads may go off by themselves to explore the surrounding area. This was in his last year at kindergarten.

Paul remembered this view when I showed it to him, recalling many happy days exploring the area with his friends.

Paul remembers also that he did have many friends but in the camp all his friends were of German nationality.

Mother and Paul often went into Arys to go shopping, visiting the post office or for the young boy to attend Kindergarten. Going on local walks, it was a popular area for rambling, and later attending school, the young Paul became used to going out and returning to the camp under guard, after all there was a war on!

Paul recalls that there was a minimum of 4 guards on duty at the gates of the garrison camp because of the presence of vast numbers of soldiers in the camp, both day and night. Mother and son were always advised to walk on the pavements in case there were any tanks coming along the street

The German soldiers always saluted the German children when they left the camp and again on their return. The old post card showing soldiers standing to attention and being inspected by a senior officer is one of Paul's most vivid memories.

Partie am Arys See Verlobungsinsel

Verlobungsinsel — Aryssee

This is a picture of the lake where Lydia taught Paul to swim in his early childhood.

Paul recalls:

"Leaving the garrison at Arys required special permission. We had to go out through the guarded gate. I remember on my birthday, that we had been out to town and on our return to the camp we had to stop outside the gate. The officer in charge told the four soldiers to stand to attention with their weapons on their shoulders and to salute. This was followed by the singing of happy birthday, 'Herzlichen Glückwunsch zum Geburtstagin,' in German of course. I was really pleased."

Paul recalls that when there were birthdays, most of the children in the same class went to each other's houses for parties. He remembers festivals in the town when friends went as a group. How times have not changed!

There were also military parades through the town, often at weekends with marching military bands.

Living on a military base, Paul couldn't fail to notice the armoured tanks and other vehicles, German as well as captured Russian T24 and T34 which were on open display on the parade ground for the purposes of training and recognition.

Paul also saw the new German battle tank, the Tiger on the street in Arys.

This is one of the entrances, possibly the main one at Arys Camp.

In these early years, Paul acquired his love of German and now British military music. At the age of 6, in 1942, he left kindergarten to attend a local junior school in the town which was a short distance from the camp. In Nazi Germany, children began school at about age 6-7 in a primary school which was called a Volks-schule (peoples' school). All children attended the Volks-schule for the first four years.

The school day began in the classroom with a "Heil Hitler" salute. When the teacher entered the classroom, the students all stood up and saluted. Children encountering their teacher on the street were also expected to give this salute.

Paul probably wore short pants and knee socks or he may have worn long stockings. Many parents let the boys wear long pants during the winter which were quite severe in East Prussia.

There were good times at school, particularly, games and school sports days, when Paul's talent as a runner first began to develop and which later blossomed in England when Paul ran for his County. He still has those treasured medals but remains very modest as to his running achievements.

Like all children who enjoyed playing games, the circumstances of the time will have influenced the contents of the games and who were the 'goodies' and the 'baddies'. With the war in full swing, children played army games but some of the German children had to take on the role of the Russians, the big bad enemy. Paul didn't mention whether the British were regarded as enemies in these games!

In the classroom, only German was spoken at the school, there was a large picture of Adolf Hitler above the blackboard and the children were taught from an early age to say Onkel, Adolf. From time to time all children had to stand and raise their right arm in the Hail Hitler, Heil Hitler in German. On April 20, Hitler's birthday, there was much saluting and singing of "Deutschland, Deutschland, uber alles," (Germany, Germany over all). Paul remembers this happening for the three years he attended the school.

It is clear that had Paul not left school at 8, to become a refugee, he would have been destined to join the Hitler Youth Movement as a member of the 'Jungvolk' when he reached the age of 10.

At ten years of age, German boys entered the 'Deutsches Jungvolk', a younger sort of Hitler Youth which I understand was similar to the Boy Scouts movement of today.

The Deutsches Jungvolk in der Hitler Jugend, German for "German Youngsters in the Hitler Youth") was the separate section for boys aged 8 to 14 of the Hitler Youth organisation in Nazi Germany. Through a programme of outdoor activities, parades and sports, it aimed to indoctrinate its young members in the tenets of Nazi ideology. Membership became fully compulsory for eligible boys in 1939. By the end of World War II, some had even become child soldiers. After the end of the war in 1945, the Deutsches Jungvolk and its parent organization, the Hitler Youth, ceased to exist.

Source of photo*: by kind permission of the museum of the former German Army HQ in Berlin, where the main protagonists involved in the unsuccessful attempt on Hitler's life, in the meeting room at the Wolf's Lair in 1944, were executed.*

Beneath the Hitler Youth were several organisations for younger boys and girls. Pimpf was the most junior branch, membership being open to boys between the ages of six and ten. Pimpf boys had a separate uniform and the organisation had its own manual dating from 1934 called 'Pimpf on Duty,' as shown below. The heavily illustrated book of 348 pages contains everything the youngest member of the Hitler Youth in the German Third Reich, the Pimpf in the Jungvolk, had to know in order to fit into the system.

Explained are lots of sports exercises, shooting, rifles training, activities out in the field like how to read a compass and read music, how to interpret a map, tying knots, how to make and erect a tent, start a fire, etc., the book even gives information on the discounts for Jungvolk members when buying tickets for public transportation.

They also completed community service, a variety of physical activities and outdoor skills such as camping. It is very likely that, although Paul has never mentioned being a Pimf boy, this is probably where he obtained his love for PE. Like their comrades in the Hitler Youth, members of Pimpf were also subjected to lessons about Nazi values and political views. They had to memorise the group's handbook, Pimpf im Dienst ('Young Ones in Service') and pass exams before 'graduating'. At age ten, Pimpf members could join the Jungvolk, before moving on to the Hitler Youth. By this time Paul had fortunately left Arys.

Shown on this page is a photograph of a school classroom. I am not sure which groups these lads were in before they joined the Hitler youth. It is terrible to know that a number of these young people became child soldiers and even faced Russian tanks on the front line in street to street battles in the centre of Berlin in 1945.Now back to Arys

Source: Reichsjugendführung / scanned by Benutzer:Wefo; edited by user Jaybear.

The location of Arys and the garrison camp less than 35 miles from the then Polish border and approximately 50 miles from the then Russian border, had encouraged some of the market stalls and smaller shops in the town to be occupied by Polish traders. A number of these also lived in Arys and some of their children attended the same kindergarten and school as Paul. In the years 1942 to early 1944, Paul enjoyed the friendship of both Polish and Jewish children. Paul didn't mention whether there was any animosity shown towards Jewish children.

The days during the war were often very exciting for a young German lad and his friends. One Sunday school was interrupted by sirens going off as Russian planes were expected and soon flew over Arys. Paul was about seven at the time and the response to the sirens was a quick sprint to the bomb shelter in the cemetery behind the church. There was a race between Paul and his friends to see who would be first to the shelter. On our trip to Paul's birthplace, we tried to find this cemetery but to no avail, perhaps it had been built over!

When I asked Paul if he could remember any of the names of his school friends there was a blank look on his face. But suddenly, after a few moments in thought his face lit up and he said:

Could this postcard overleaf be of the actual cycle shop referred to in the paragraphs below, I wonder.

"Ah yes, you're not going to believe this but at the moment only one name comes to mind, Anita Weinke." Trust him, I thought.

After probing a bit more we discovered that the Cieka and Weinke families knew each other quite well. It seems that Lydia Cieka was a bit of a cyclist and often cycled from the army camp into Arys. When her bike needed some attention she would visit the Weinke's cycle repair shop. Paul can't recall having a bike when he was a young boy. A bike shop is shown is shown on the old Arys map as number 52 on page 103. Surely there was only one bike shop in a town of the size of Arys?

Later, he does remember some friends from kindergarten and junior school which include Anita Weinke, and a number of other girls- Hannelore, Ruth, Gisela, Steffie, Elizabeth and Karen. For the boys there was Siegfried, Otto, Karl and Isaak who was probably Jewish and the son of a market trader. There was also Hubert and two brothers Dieter and Siegfried Reckling, sons of a Lutheran Minister, who later went to Tanganika Hubert possibly could have been Hubert Jockwitz, as recalled by my German friend Dietrich Peylo who knew a Hubert of about Paul's age, but who died recently. Dietrich's brother was born in 1937 so he may have known Paul as well.

A postcard of the cycle shop in Arys.

Although there was no mention of a bike for Paul, he did have a transportation interest and that was trains.

Trains have always featured in Paul's life and even today he has a collection of model trains and likes nothing better than to ride with his wife Lynn on the little trains of Wales, especially the one from Portmadog in North Wales.

Back in the 1940s, Paul senior wanted to take his son to see the steam trains but it seems that Paul was too scared to go because of the noise.

It appeared that the main railway line passed near to Arys with trains of soldiers going to Poland and especially Russia to fight on the eastern front. Later, Paul, fascinated by the steam engines, would be taken by his grandparents to watch the trains returning and to see the wounded soldiers on board. In particular, Paul would notice the last few carriages of each train would have the curtains drawn shut out of respect as they were in fact carrying the coffins of dead soldiers.

The ever inquisitive Paul would ask:

"Why are the curtains drawn?" But no answer was given as I suspect it was thought that to tell the truth might be too upsetting for the young child.

Later, when Paul must have been a little older in early 1944, his uncle, Arnold suggested that he take his nephew to see the trains. This time the truth was revealed as Paul learnt that the carriages with windows closed and curtains drawn "were full of boxes of dead soldiers returning presumably from the Russian front." This was at Stalluponen when Paul was visiting his grandparents, having taken a trip by train from Arys station.

....
....

No record of Paul's early life would be complete without reference to his parents and his ancestry.

The two families have been traced back to Paul's grandparents. On the paternal side, the Cieka family, it may have been Ciecka then a Polish name, Paul and Elise, (nee Richnau) came from Konigsberg, later changed in 1946 to Kaliningrad after the war having fallen into Russian hands on 9th April when the German garrison surrendered to the Soviets.

On the maternal side, were Johann and August Schroder (nee Paulukat) who were from Stalluponen, later re-named in 1938 as Ebnenrode.

The town was later overrun by the Soviet Red Army during World War II on January 13, 1945. The region was transferred from Germany to the Russian SFSR in 1945 and made a part of Kaliningrad Oblast. In 1946, the town, whose German inhabitants had been largely evacuated or expelled westward, was renamed Nesterov after Sergey Nesterov, a Soviet war hero who was killed in the vicinity.

Paul remembers travelling by train to go on holidays to visit both grandparents. The Schroders were a family of five, Hans, Erich, Lydia (our Paul's mum who married Paul Cieka), Paul and Arnold. The family business was bespoke tailoring and cutting. Lydia worked in Arys as a shop assistant in Kaisers' confectioner's shop selling coffee amongst other items. Please see map and list of properties, number 55 on pages 45 and 46.

Interestingly, the German last name Schröder or Schroeder is an occupational name for a tailor or cutter of cloth, from the Middle Low German schroden or schraden, meaning "to cut."

Herr and Frau Cieka had a son, Paul (our Paul's dad), a daughter Lilli, a third child, a daughter, who our Paul never met and who left the family in disgrace, Paul thinks in her teens or early twenties. A bit of a mystery clearly!

Surprisingly, the Ciekas seem to have engaged in a similar occupation to the Schroders. They were bespoke tailors and cutters and working from rooms at home.

Interestingly, Paul believes that the Schroders and the Ciekas met in Konisberg at the Ciekas' house on a business trip and it is thought that this is where Lydia met Paul senior who was home on leave from the army, having volunteered for army service in the early1930s. They were married in1935.

It seems that the proximity of Stalluponen to the Russian border prompted a family decision to persuade the maternal grandparents to move further west in East Prussia to Preusish or Prussian Holland.

With the arrival of the Red Army in early 1945 and the end of the war, Preußisch Holland became part of the People's Republic of Poland. It was renamed Pasłęk and the surviving ethnic Germans were expelled.

Unfortunately and sadly, both grandparents were captured by the Russians with Paul's maternal grandad sent to Siberia, whilst his grandma was made to work for a Polish family.

Grandad was brought back from the Siberian labour camp to be reunited with his wife, but died shortly after his return. Grandmother, also not in the best of health, was later put on a train as a stretcher case to Wuppertal, Germany. Before I continue, here is a bit of history about Wuppertal.

From July 5, 1933 to January 19, 1934, the Kemna concentration camp was established in Wuppertal. It was one of the early Nazi concentration camps, created by the Third Reich to incarcerate their political opponents after the Nazi Party first gained power in 1933. The camp was established in a former factory on the river Wupper.

During World War II, about 40% of buildings in the city were destroyed by Allied bombing, as were many other German cities and industrial centres.

The US 78th Infantry Division under Major general Edwin P. Parker Jr. captured Wuppertal against scant resistance on April 16, 1945. Wuppertal became a part of the British Zone of Occupation, and subsequently part of the new state of North Rhine-Westphalia in West Germany. Now back to life with the Ciekas post World War II.

Lydia Cieka received a message whilst in Denmark in 1948, that grandmother Schroder was in a care home in Schwelm in the western part of Germany in the Ruhr and so decided to make her home in the same town when she was able to leave Denmark with Paul's brother Hans Peter.

Elise Cieka (nee Richau) was born on 25/07/1874 in Wehlau, East Prussia and died in Konigsburg on 21/09/1945.

A family tree has been prepared, as far as it has been able to trace the family history, to discern the family connections with the information available showing Paul's ancestors and his relations. This is contained in Appendix 1 of this book.

From looking at the Ciekas' family history and what happened to some of them during WW2, we move to consider the effect on East Prussia of the Soviet advance westwards in 1944 and the resulting impact on the population of the military town of Arys.

Chapter 3

The Russians are coming

"The Russians are coming" is a phrase attributed to United States Secretary of Defence, James Forrestal in 1949. In full, Forrestal said "The Russians are coming. The Russians are coming. They're right around. I've seen Russian soldiers."

Forrestal allegedly uttered those words while suffering from mental illness, not long before purportedly committing suicide.

There is also the addition which goes – "The Russians are coming, send reinforcements we are going to advance or send three and four pence we are going to a dance." The origin of this may be attributed to poor army communication, lost in the annals of time.

What is clear however, in our story, is that in 1944, during World War II, the German army was in retreat as the Eastern Front approached the East Prussian border with the Soviet army certainly advancing westwards. The Russians were definitely coming and the effect on the resident German population was very dramatic, a very hasty preparation to flee westwards with as much as could be carried, or loaded on carts, or on bicycles.

Soviet soldiers had pushed on into south-east Prussia by October 1944. During the winter of 1944/1945, they gained considerable ground and advanced through the rest of East Prussia, Pomerania and West Prussia, cutting off the Eastern Territories from the rest of the fatherland.

At this time, Paul and his mum felt the full weight of the German propaganda machine. The German High Command and Adolf Hitler continually poured out news on the radio that there was absolutely nothing to be concerned about or have fears about the future in the Russian theatre of war. The message for home consumption was that Germany was certainly winning the war!

In fact, Hitler, who installed himself as the supreme German military leader or Fuhrer, was warned repeatedly by his commanders that a Soviet offensive in the east was coming. He called the Red Army 'the greatest bluff since Genghis Khan' and chose to ignore the advice, to his great cost.

The reality appeared to be somewhat different as there were many stories coming from the hospital on the Arys army camp from young wounded soldiers that 'the war was not going so well.' The accounts from the young soldiers were based on what they had seen and experienced first- hand. These young men were being patched up and then sent back to the Eastern front for action. Paul remembered seeing the wounded soldiers on trains coming back from the Russian front.

Paul recalls that there was talking at school that the Russians had reached Johannisberg some 15 miles south west of Arys.

Unfortunately, the people of East Prussia received no warning and were caught by surprise when the Soviet troops actually arrived on the doorstep. Even though local German military commanders had, weeks in advance, asked to evacuate the civilian population, Hitler had rejected their requests. He confirmed the need for every German to stand their ground to defend the fatherland.

Despite the words of Adolf Hitler, Lydia didn't believe for one minute that German troops would be coming to protect them from the Russians advancing west. She decided very wisely to take matters into her own hands. In fact, it seems that not everybody believed in the Nazi lies that East Prussia was safe. Could it be that Paul senior was surely one of these? Perhaps, in his position, he probably had more up-to-date information about the Russian advance and could he have been in contact with his wife urging the family to move westward to a safer area?

Gauleiter or Head of the administrative district of Königsberg, Erich Koch, even when the Soviets were already in East Prussia, decreed that only people who lived in the east of the province could evacuate, while promising to the others that there was no danger and they should stay put. Koch however, worked frantically to secure his own evacuation by ship. When he left the city, he ordered the crew to bar the ship to any other refugee even though the ship had plenty of space to take on many others. Typical, I thought, just like a rat to leave a sinking ship or in his case East Prussia!

Often it was known for the German army to facilitate the flight of the refugees despite the contrary orders of the Nazi Party. In other cases however, the same Wehrmacht actually made it difficult for the refugees as we shall see in the next chapter by clearing them off roads to enable soldiers and vehicles to pass quickly so that they could escape the Russian advance.

What needs to be understood and recognised is that, at this time, there was chaos and confusion often mixed with great fear and hysteria as, with no reliable information, people didn't know what was happening. Rumours spread like wildfire and people naturally enough panicked. They just had to leave and organise their own departure as there were no plans for an orderly evacuation of the civilian population.

It is estimated that around as many as three to four million Germans fled the advance of the Red Army prior to the end of the war.

According to Dietrich Peylo, in his postcards book of Arys, assuming of course that I have translated the German in a reasonable fashion, the town of Arys, largely spared by the war until the middle of January 1945, witnessed a dreary calm. It was the propaganda, threats and the failure of the German Reich and those responsible, which prevented a legitimate evacuation of the civilian population. As the Soviet front approached, a chaotic movement of flight by many of the residents began in earnest.

The last train left Arys station on January 22nd 1945, not a moment too soon as the bombardment of the city, which until then had remained largely intact, took place. Forty houses went up in flames; the town hall, the Orchard building the seat of the parish, the headquarters and two barracks were lost. Although there is still some uncertainty as to the cause of the destruction as, soon after the Soviet occupation on 23 January 1945, many houses burned down, perhaps because of the use of candle lights.

Many residents left it too late to begin their trek away from Arys. The weather was terrible and the departing refugees were hampered by snow and ice and all the traffic routes from the town were severely congested. Those who could not escape were soon exposed to the roughest treatment. A number of the remaining inhabitants were shot, Dietrich Peylo, my contact in Germany and author of the Postcards of Arys book, heard. It seems that even the wearing of military-looking boots, for instance, was a sufficient reason. Dietrich's Aunt Lydia told him that a particular Soviet officer took measures to protect civilians but we don't know what these were. But still these civilians had to leave Arys some weeks later.

Those residents that remained had to share the remaining facilities with those refugees coming from the East, many of them, just like the Ciekas and the Peylos lost everything.

It is well known that many millions living in eastern parts of Germany or German settlements in different East and South East states fled or were expelled. According to Dietrich Peylo, "many hundreds of thousands of civilians were abused, or deported into the Soviet Union for forced labour or lost their lives."

For Arys, the Soviet Intelligence Service, NKVD, set up an internment camp in the grounds of the former German army base in part of the barracks. In August 1945, the city was handed over to the Polish authorities, who gave it the old Mazovian name of Orzysz.

Mazovia is a historical region in mid-north-eastern Poland. It spans the North European Plain, roughly between Lodz and Bialystok, with Warsaw being the unofficial capital and largest city. Throughout the centuries, Mazovia developed a separate sub-culture featuring diverse folk songs, architecture, dress and traditions different from those of other Poles. Historical Mazovia existed from the Middle Ages until the partitions of Poland.

On October 23rd 1945 in Orzysz, of the approximately 400 people remaining or returning, 300 were expelled, who didn't want to stay in Poland. We now return to 1944.

Having looked at what happened in the town of Arys as the Soviet army pushed westwards in east Prussia we now begin to turn out attention to the Ciekas personal escape from the town in 1944 by considering what happened in particular in December 1944 and what it was that lead to the departure of the Ciekas from the military town of Arys.

Chapter 4

'The Great Escape'

'The Great Escape', from the tunnel of Harry out of Stalag Luft III, of 73 prisoners of war, on 24th March 1944, in the upper Silesia province of Germany, now near the town of Zagan in Poland, has spawned two major films, numerous TV documentaries and two books to my knowledge and has been well publicised. It is even possible to visit the site today which my wife Sue and I did in June 2018. What a fascinating place with an amazing museum and a very helpful curator. More of this later!

Individual accounts of refugees escaping from East Prussia from the advancing Soviet army are less well known but no less worthy of mention as I hope this story will demonstrate.

As it became fairly obvious that an Allied victory was going to happen and following the battle of Stalingrad, during the Russian advance into East Prussia in 1944/1945, many thousands of German citizens, mainly women and children, fled westwards away from advancing troops. By October 1944, Soviet soldiers had reached the border of East Prussia and during the following harsh winter, the Red Army conquered the rest of East Prussia, Pomerania and West Prussia effectively severing the link between the Eastern territories and the remainder of Germany.

The 'East Prussian Offensive' was a strategic offensive by the Red Army against the German Wehrmacht on the Eastern Front. It lasted from 13 January 1945 to 25 April 1945, though some German units did not surrender until 9 May. The Battle of Königsberg was a major part of the offensive, which ended with a total victory for the Red Army.

Few of the evacuations were organised before the Russians arrived. More commonly, Germans fled on horse drawn carts or simply walked or cycled. The key concern was to avoid contact with representatives of the Red army at all cost.

As to the men folk, the great majority including Paul senior, were away from home and engaged in defending the Fatherland or in other occupations linked to the war effort.

Those leaving East Prussia often only took the clothing they were wearing and what they could manage to carry in bags, school satchels and rucksacks. Others who perhaps had more time to organise their escape left on agricultural carts or farm wagons, some even left on trains from Arys station. Many just walked clutching their belongings. It must have been a desperate and very frightening experience for those involved.

Paul recalls that one night, he doesn't remember the exact date, sometime during the very cold winter of 1944, may be December, just before Christmas, he and his mother were just having their supper, when they had cause to quickly pack up and leave the Arys Camp.

The meal he and his mother were eating was his special favourite, erbsen suppe (pea soup) with the everlasting German bratwurst sausage floating on the surface of the saucepan.

Suddenly, there was shouting outside in the street below. Their flat must have overlooked the street, even though they lived on the army camp, and so his mother, Lydia, opened the window to see and hear what all the commotion was about.

The voices that came from below were:

"Flee for your lives the Russians are upon us, they are on the edge of our town, hurry, hurry."

We don't know quite the location of the Russians at this time but they can't have been far away as Arys town centre was only a short distance from the camp.

This map is included with the kind permission of Dietrich Peylo and it shows the places the Ciekas were intending to reach or the towns that did reach from Arys-, dotted circle, on their trek towards Danzig (Gdansk)-middle left via the Frisches Haff- to the right of Danzig. After Danzig they still had a long way to go to reach safety and Flensborg for a ship to Denmark.

Mother and son quickly found their warmest winter clothing and hurried downstairs into the street. Paul remembers it was snowing outside.

Lydia had previously warned her son that someday they may have to leave the camp urgently but it was still a great shock when that day actually dawned.

So Mother and her eight year old son left the army base with crowds of other Germans leaving the town to begin what would become their long march which would take them eventually to the Danish border many weeks later. Their previously warm and secure home, so they thought, and the contents, indeed everything, was left behind, with the evening's supper on the table and Paul's toys remaining.

Paul has mentioned to me that there were Christmas presents that were made by French and Italian prisoners of war, some of whom worked in the officers' kitchen at the camp. A common name was Franz. All the Christmas presents, much to Paul's dismay, were left behind.

Paul reminisces about three Christmases at Arys. He wished to stress to me that it is important to remember that most countries in Europe have three days which are very special at Christmas. The most important day for the Germans is Hailiger Abend or Holy Evening, which we know as Christmas Eve, followed by two days of celebration which included family visits.

Christmas Eve in fact is very important to Germans because this is when the Weihnachtsman (Father Christmas) visits, if possible with presents (pre-arranged with the family) in his sack. If that is not possible, he leaves the presents but these are smaller items such as toys, sweets and fruit which are left on the Bunte Teller. In the Germany of the 1940s this would be a coloured plate, card board in days gone by, but today it is probably plastic.

There were also Christmas Eve trips to the Lutheran church in the centre of Arys to sing carols. Paul was in trouble one Christmas Eve in church as he seemed to have been given a watch by his father. Not content with just admiring the new time piece, he seemed to want to fiddle with the winder. After some time, mum Lydia must have become exasperated with her son's fiddling during the service, as Paul recalls the following short sharp conversation with Lydia.

"Paul do you want the Weihnactsman to come?"

"Oh, yes," says Paul quickly stopping the fiddling, worried that Weihnactsman wouldn't come!

Living in a garrison camp in officers' quarters, it is more than likely that a trainee officer would have been given the task of fulfilling the role of Weihnactsman.

There would certainly be no stockings which according to Paul, resident of the UK "is a very special English custom and long may it flourish!!"

When Paul was very young, he remembers the excitement when a proper pine tree was delivered to their home and was fully decorated before Christmas Eve. Amazingly, when we think of today's health and safety regulations, real wax candles were affixed to the branches with little cups/plates to catch any surplus which may have dripped down when the candles were alight.

I asked Paul about Christmas lunch and his memory is of eating duck and chicken but he was unable to say any more.

We don't know if the stories of the atrocities committed by Russian soldiers on the existing population, particularly women and children, as they advanced west in East Prussia, which had filtered through to the camp, were all true. We are not sure what Lydia Cieka knew. But it was clearly sensible for the fleeing Ciekas and other Germans, fearful of their lives, to avoid meeting any soldiers from the Soviet Army.

We now know that the Russians had decided to take their revenge on the German population. This was for the past atrocities committed by German soldiers on Russians as the Germans advanced east earlier in the war.

"Many Germans who had access to newspapers and radio broadcasts were aware that the Soviets were pressing in on East Prussia and many Germans saw newsreel footage or heard reports of the atrocities which occurred in villages such as Nemmersdorf." ('Germans displaced from the East: Crossing Actual and Imagined Central European Borders, 1944-1955', Amy A Alrich 2003).

Mother and son commenced the walk in warm coats, fur hats and scarfs and their stieffels (German for boots), leaving the snow bound officers' quarters. Joining the ever growing column of refugees, the plan was to make their way round the Masuren Lakes, and continue through the town of Arys and past several lakes in a straight line travelling through a rural area dominated by agriculture and forestry away from East Prussia, by passing Lotzen towards and through Osrterode (Ostrod).

The town of Lotzen was occupied by the Soviet Union's Red Army in 1945 during World War II and placed under Polish administration after the war ended. The German-speaking populace who had not been evacuated during the war were subsequently expelled westward. The town was renamed Giżycko in 1946 in honour of the Masurian folklorist Gustaw Gizewiusz, a 19th-century Evangelical-Lutheran pastor in southern East Prussia, who had greatly supported Polish language and Polish culture

The Ciekas really wished to reach Preushiss Holland (Paslek) to check on the welfare of the maternal grandparents. As they continued on their way to Ebling (Eblag), they were diverted from there because of fighting ahead and so had to head towards the University City of Konigsberg, later renamed Kaliningrad by the Russians. The aim this time was to check on the welfare of the paternal grandparents. Once again they were thwarted in their attempt to visit their relatives by further fighting.

The Ciekas were accompanied by other Germans with carts and cattle. There were several thousands of people on this mass trek of refugees heading westwards. The hope was that the fortunes of the German army might change for the better and the refugees might be able to return to their villages, towns and cities to resume their daily lives. As things turned out this was not to be.

Some of the refugees had also fled from other areas occupied by Russians as they advanced west. There were also wounded men and women who had suffered injuries as a result of air raids.

During the first night, after some kilometres of walking, Lydia and Paul, found a barn along a road and sheltered there for the night. Often though there was no shelter and they simply had to sleep by the side of the road. Paul has told me that he was often very tired on the walk and whenever they passed a forest he wanted to lie down and go to sleep. Lydia was often torn between the need for her son to sleep and the urgency of keeping on the move away from the advancing Russians.

Sadly in the days that followed, Paul saw, for the first time, the dead bodies of adults, principally women and children who had collapsed and died on the roadside, in ditches and in fields with no-one to remove or bury them.

Whilst on the march, an elderly man took the 8 years old Paul by the hand to help with a job that needed doing. Unfortunately there were the bodies of children lying on the road, often in the middle, or in a ditch at the side where they had collapsed and died. Paul was asked to help in their relocation to the side of the road or onto adjacent land. Hopefully they would be buried later.

The photo is probably not of the Ciekas but definitely of refugees fleeing from the Russians; note the snow on the ground and the clothes they are wearing and all their belongings. Source: Budesarchiv and photographer: Blaschka. Date of photo: Winter 1945.

Paul's specific task, which must have been really awful and unimaginable for one so young, was to hold each child's head still while the body was moved. Paul recalls that those helping simply wanted to move the children to a better place so that they would not be trampled on by soldiers or crushed by passing military vehicles often retreating from the advancing Russians.

Paul remembers a worried Mum shouting: "Hurry up Paul."

There is another incident which weighs heavily on Paul's memory.

As I have said, it was often necessary for mother and son to dive into a roadside ditch to escape military vehicles which had priority on the road. In case there was any doubt as to what the refugees should do, there were angry cries of "Schnell, Schnell" (hurry up) from German soldiers passing them on the trek.

One particular day mother and son, Paul did not know the location, were shivering and sheltering at the bottom of a snow filled ditch because of the nearby artillery fire which could have been either German or Russian.

Suddenly, without warning, the first shell hit a barn and farmhouse on the far side of the road and there was an almighty explosion and subsequent fire. The next shell landed somewhere between the farmhouse and where the Ciekas were crouched with hands over their ears but was definitely nearer. Lydia, a good Lutheran shouted to Paul, "put your hands together and pray." Hoping that a third shell would not land in the ditch, it was their good fortune that they survived the onslaught and continued unharmed on their journey. I am sure that somebody was looking out for them! The prayers had been answered! This encouraged them to get off the road.

This particular picture overleaf shows streams of refugees being kept to one side of the road, with soldiers also walking. Note the vehicle tracks. The photo is dated Winter 1945. Source: Bundesarchive, photographer: O. Ang.

I am sure the Ciekas would have walked in a similar fashion in a refugee convoy like this through the forest as in the photograph above.

Another occasion Paul remembers, unfortunately because of more recent flashbacks, is an incident when Mother Nature called but obviously there was no toilet conveniently available, please excuse the pun! Lydia told Paul to nip behind a hedge, possibly into a graveyard, Paul recalls.

Regrettably, what Paul found, no adult would want to witness, never mind a young and impressionable lad. For what Paul encountered was the heavily mutilated body of a young woman. Paul remembers the detailed picture and has told me the gory details but I am not going to describe them here. Suffice to say the Russians had got there first!

There were further hardships to bear on route. The Ciekas had left Arys in a hurry and so had not been able to take many clothes. So Lydia also had to use her inherited skills of tailoring and had to become part of the 'make and mend' brigade as she constantly adapted their clothing whilst on the move, which was particularly important to stave off the cold of a very bad winter.

Also they saw German and Russian motorised vehicles damaged, burnt out and even totally destroyed. The 8 year old German boy Paul wondered what had happened to the crews/occupants of those vehicles large and small. No one will ever know.

The snake–like column of refugees were led by self-appointed, ex-service men and generally marched between the German and Russian lines and usually on country roads, often passing troops and tanks.

Paul recalls:

"There were three occasions when I clearly remember that there were men travelling with the group who were each wearing a military belt. They must have been German deserters. One I think was an NCO."

Lydia Cieka would take her son to one side and quietly say again and again-"I am sorry Paul, this is war, please hurry up, we must keep up and walk."

As the walk continued and the Ciekas talked to other refugees it was clear that quite a lot of Polish people were also escaping the advancing Russians.

This connection with Polish people provides me with an opportunity to explain that the name Cieka had not been the original family name which was in fact Ciecka. Shortly after mother and son became refugees, Lydia was strongly advised to remove the letter "C" in their surname. This is because they could be mistaken for being Polish or Jewish and Polish people were not welcome or popular. As for Jewish people they would probably fear for their lives if caught by the Nazis.

The next significant place that our weary travellers approached was the town of Wormditt (Orneta) only they didn't reach the town itself. They were stopped west of Wormditt, a town where the Jewish community suffered terribly from Anti-Semitism, by German troops who insisted they went north to Frisches Haff. (Zaleu Wastany). The aim was to leave East Prussia by crossing the frozen bays which formed the natural coastline.

As it was a bitterly cold winter, with the travelling conditions extremely severe, mother decided that, having already walked many miles, to go back would be too dangerous so, with many others, they should make their way on to the frozen Frisches Haff. They must have desperate to attempt a crossing!

This was a brackish water lagoon on the Baltic Sea, fifty six miles long, six to fifteen miles wide and seventeen foot deep!

As a result of the Russian advance, they became stranded on the shores of the Frisches Haff. At any other time of the year many hundreds of the refugees would have been captured by the Russians.

"As all road and railway connections to the rest of Germany were severed, the treks of refugees were forced to cross the frozen Frisches Haff to the Frisches Nehrung, a land spit or peninsula to the city of Danzig (Gdansk). Hundreds of thousands of refugees streamed across the frozen sea at great danger not only from the constant Soviet shelling and air attacks but also because the ice gave way under the weight of wagons and people.

Added to the hardship of the refugees, the winter of 1944/1945 was one of the severest on record. The temperature dropped to minus 20 degrees C to minus 30 degrees C. All roads were ice and snow bound leading to many deaths from freezing, particularly among older people and young children." ('Forgotten Voices, the expulsion of the Germans from Eastern Europe after World War II, Ulrich Merten, 2013).

It seemed that the Soviet Air Force had no scruples about bombing the refugees. Any good weather with clear skies the bombers came without mercy causing huge explosions and big holes in the ice and many refugees lost their lives by a direct hit or drowning in the freezing water. Many others lay prostrate on the ice hoping they would be saved. This was all in vain as no rescue by the German authorities was possible.

Snow storms were also frequent occurrences. These are storms characterized by a significant volume of snow with accompanying high wind which may last a long time.

The location of this photo is unknown. It could be the Frisches Haff or just refugees in convoy crossing frozen ground in terrible winter conditions of

1945, the same conditions that the Ciekas would have suffered. It looks grim, particularly in black and white!

Source: Bundesarchiv

However, Frisches Haff was fortunately frozen with thick ice and Paul and Mum intended to cross over the ice reaching the strip of land on the other side to Nehrung and leading on to Gdansk (Danzig).Unfortunately, Paul remembers clearly that:

"The Russians were bombing the ice, every day, to hold up the movement of German troops and many fleeing east Prussians drowned in the icy waters during that winter."

I am not sure but it is likely that the Ciekas crossed between Heiligenbeil and Braunsberg, possibly as recorded by Nicolas Stargardt in his excellent book, 'Witnesses of War:'

"Within range of Soviet artillery, they set out at night, the farmers driving their carts in single file over routes marked by occasional torches and with improvised bridges strung across the stretches where the ice had broken up". ('Witnesses of War', Childrens Lives Under the Nazis, Nicolasl Stargardt, 2005.)

Paul has very vivid memories of the horrible sights and sounds walking over the ice. He had never heard a horse scream before but many did as they crashed through the icy into the watery depths below. Unfortunately, some areas of ice had thawed or melted as they had been bombed by the Russians and were breaking up with the freezing water coming to the surface.

I have seen photographs in the book by Ulrich Merten of the slow moving treks of refugees and it looked like the long column of a funeral procession, all the more vivid because the photos were black and white. What a desperate situation for a young boy and his mother to endure!

Lydia tried to reassure Paul that the horses would have lost consciousness very quickly and so should not have suffered too much. I am not sure he was convinced!

Lydia, also at times, had to be emotionally very strong to protect her son.

"Paul, you have to be very brave and very good and I won't hit you unless you do something bad."

This was a comment which would be criticised today but these times in the 1940s in war were very hard and very different and may have required a different approach by a parent as the only way of getting through the day.

Paul remembers this warning but can't recall whether it was a reference to the following incident.

It was clear that there was a crossing point over the frozen Haff and there was a long queue of refugees passing and waiting to cross. There was also a rumour, as people passed the waiting Ciekas, that there was another crossing further down the Haff. We all know how quickly rumours can spread especially when lives are threatened and people start to panic!

As Paul started to shiver from the cold, he pleaded with mum.

"I want to go to the other crossing," he cried out.

But Lydia stood firm and was not to be persuaded and calmly replied that they must stay here and wait their turn to cross the bridge. We don't know what happened to the refugees who decided to attempt the other crossing.

As they walked on gingerly over the ice, they came across a second huge break in the ice. Lydia walking beside Paul urged him:

"Don't look or stare, I don't want you to see all the floating corpses, schau links." This was an urgent instruction to look left.

Photograph overleaf supplied by kind permission of RH Permissions from Forgotten Voices of the Second World War by Max Arthur- Refugees Crossing frozen Frisches Haff, East Prussia, 1944/1945.

Fortunately, for the Ciekas, help was at hand in the form of the German army which built a wooden bridge over the fractured ice and mother and son were able to walk down the thin strip of land with the hope of reaching Danzig. Unfortunately not all the refugees crossed without incident and indeed some of the farmers' carts didn't make the journey as they were too heavy to cross and so sunk into the watery depths.

Unfortunately following one of our discussions, some months later, as Paul was reading a book entitled 'We the last Children of Ostpreussens (East Prussia), a Forgotten Generation', where all the contributors were children, like Paul, he began to suffer some nightmares at his home in Crewe.

In another one of his wonderful letters to me he writes:

".....Recently almost every night my sleep was disturbed because in flashbacks I was back at Frisches Haff in the queue for the only temporary wooden bridge across a large gap in the ice. I relived seeing overloaded farm carts often horse-drawn losing balance and falling into the open water on either side and what haunted and kept me awake were the drowning panic stricken horses. I have never forgotten the terrifying noises and clutching my mother's hand although, only eight years old, realising that there was nothing we could do."

Having crossed the bridge, the large group of walking refugees were split, leaving mother and son as part of a small group of 20, mainly mums and children plus two elderly gentlemen who had dropped behind the main column. They were resting in a clearing in the forest. Suddenly, out of nowhere, there appeared a squad of Russian soldiers, wearing fur caps, about 6-9 men in uniform with machine guns who soon surrounded the group. They were shouting 'Soldaten, soldaten, uniform, uniform.

Paul recalls. "They were obviously suspicious of us."

I asked Paul to explain the Russians behaviour and he thought that they were looking for German deserters. The leader of the patrol waved to the fearful Germans to sit down as the soldiers rested their machine guns on their laps.

The Russians had certainly moved west and north very rapidly.

The group was questioned for 4 hours, more likely interrogated, to see if there were any German soldiers present, any weapons or uniforms hiding underneath winter overcoats. Paul recalls:

"We dared not talk or move."

When the Russian soldiers put down their weapons, one of the elderly gentlemen shouted:

"Schnell, schnell, wald, wald wald." Quick, woods was the instruction.

They did hurry into the woods as urged by the man and "for a very long time we hid in the undergrowth." Paul wanted to call out "Mutti, Mutti,"(Mum, Mum) but he dared not for fear of giving away their position.

After a time, it seemed like ages to Paul, the same elderly man, he was about sixty, calmly spoke to the group and asked them to come out slowly as the Russians had gone. The German refugees obviously posed no threat to the might of the Red Army!

This area described by Paul as woods may have been the tree screen along the Nehrung, separating them from the harsh and biting wind coming off the Baltic sea, bordering the military road with the Frisches Haff on the left. They still had not escaped the fearful dread and danger of occasional Russian artillery shells flying overhead. It must have been terrible!

It is estimated that thousands of refugees crossed the Frisches Haff. They were hoping above all else to reach the port of Danzig to board ships which would take them to western Germany or to Denmark. They couldn't leave too soon as by the end of February 1945, the ice over the Haff was disintegrating and so this escape route was no longer available.

It is uncertain how many used this route to trek over the ice to the Nehrung and then on to Danzig," 600,000 across the Haff or along the Nehrung towards Danzig". ('Witnesses of War', Childrens' Lives Under the Nazis, Nicolas Stargardt, 2005.)

We don't know much more about the route onwards, but I suspect mother and son may have travelled to Kahlberg, (now Krynica Morska) depending on where they crossed the Haff and then on the road along the sand dunes of the Nehrung sand spit, possibly passing Stutthof concentration camp towards the port of Danzig.

Stutthof was a Nazi German concentration camp established in a secluded, wet, and wooded area near the small town of Sztutowo (German: Stutthof) 21 mies east of the city of Danzig in the former territory of the Free City of Danzig. The camp was set up around existing structures after the invasion of Poland in World War II, used for the imprisonment of Polish leaders and intelligentsia. The actual barracks were built the following year by hundreds of prisoners.

Stutthof was the first Nazi concentration camp set up outside German borders in World War II, in operation from 2 September 1939. It was also the last camp liberated by the Allies on 9 May 1945

Eventually they reached Danzig where they rested here for a few days confident of relative safety and cared for by the German Red Cross (Deutsche Rotes Kruckenkreuz) as were many refugees (photo).

Photo on previous page.Source: Budesarchiv. German refugees fleeing the Soviet Army in the Winter of 1945

The photographer was Brigette Hober.

I showed Paul the photograph on the previous page of refugees trekking through the streets of Danzig which he wasn't sure whether he remembered but he did say that he "wondered who fed the horses."

On arrival at Danzig, Lydia discovered that the trains were still running and so mother and son, with a lull in the fighting, travelled west from Danzig to Stralsrund.

During the Nazi period (1933–1945), Stralsund's military installations expanded, and a naval training base opened on the nearby island of Dänholm. In World War II the city was subjected to repeated Allied bombing. Attacks by the U.S. Army Air Forces in 1944 killed some 800 Stralsunders and destroyed an estimated 8,000 dwellings. The 354th Rifle Division of the Red Army occupied Stralsund on April 28, 1945, 10 days before the end of the war in Europe. Approximately half its population had fled.

After Stralsrund the Ciekas then went on to Sellin on the east coast of the Baltic Sea island of Ruggen. This was quite a long journey, and it must have taken a long time, looking at my modern map of the Baltic coastline, provided by Paul. Today it is over 350 miles by road and over 8 hours by fast train! I suspect it took the Ciekas much longer! What relative luxury, I expect they slept a lot in the relative warmth, out of the winter cold. Lydia must have had some money to pay for the rail fare.

They about spent 10-14 days at Sellin in a small hotel, what a change in their circumstances! Paul is unsure of the precise length of time, before they left the island on a local train, joining again the long column of hundreds of refugees travelling westwards, after leaving Ruggen via the bridge to Stralsrund. Here the refugees were escorted by German police to a school gymnasium. German police still directed the refugees from place to place and then onwards in the direction of the city of Flensburg. ID cards were checked regularly from the time the Ciekas left Arys. News also continued to be received by radio that the Russians were continuing to advance westwards.

Looking at the modern map again, it is many miles to Flensburg from Stralsrund. Paul has drawn on it a possible route via Rostock and Lubeck and Kiel, but he has not mentioned these towns in our discussions so presumably mum and son travelled by train to Flensburg. Today it is over 230 miles by modern roads and over 5 hours by fast train. I suspect it took the Ciekas much longer!

Flensburg lies at the innermost tip of the Flensburg Fjord, an inlet of the Baltic Sea. Flensburg's eastern shore is part of the Angeln peninsula.

Interestingly, in May 1945 Flensburg was the site of the last government of Nazi Germany, the so-called Flensburg government led by Karl Dönitz, which was in power from 1 May (after Hitler's death) for one week until German armies surrendered and the town was occupied by Allied troops. The regime was officially dissolved on 23 May 1945.

During the Second World War, the town was left almost unscathed by the air raids that devastated other German cities. However, in 1943, 20 children died when their nursery school was bombed, and shortly after the war ended, an explosion at a local munitions storage site claimed many victims.

The Ciekas stayed in the Flensburg area for some time, we are not sure how long but had an amazing escape from a cellar after an Allied air raid. Paul remembers:

"As long as I live I will not forget the German city of Flensburg which my mother and I were visiting, unknown to us, just before a very heavy Allied air raid. As quickly as we could we made our way to the nearest clearly marked air raid shelter, little realising at the time that what happened next was to make us refugees for a second time and bring us to southern Denmark."

Sheltering in a cellar bomb shelter, the pair heard a tremendous explosion, suddenly all the lights went out as the house above must have been hit by a bomb and then collapsed. This was followed by a gush of water draining into the very same cellar. Only it wasn't water! The pipe leading into the cellar was actually a sewage pipe, as a sewer in the road had broken. They were drenched from head to toe in an unpleasant liquid. Fortunately for them a feature of cellars in this part of the city was that they were connected to that of their neighbour by what for the Ciekas was an escape hatch. With the level of sewage rising they quickly clambered through the hole in the wall to freedom.

Unfortunately all their personal papers, identity cards, the Family Book which records important events in the family's life such marriage births, baptisms and Paul's birth certificate and other documents were destroyed in the air raid. This was to create serious problems for the Ciekas in terms of confirming their identity in the future but that is outside the scope of this story.

On reaching the street, mother and son were hosed down by a stirrup pump by the Fire Brigade and Red Cross volunteers. It must have been freezing and also quite embarrassing.

Some of the incidents Paul may have deliberately or unwittingly tried to forget but I hope the compiling of this book will help Paul to remember the memories of him and his mother as great and loving companions and even greater survivors.

There is a constant memory which he recalls from the long march from East to West. It is that they often had to beg for scraps of food. Most people would say no when asked but some kindly said "yes I have a crust for the boy." The boy was Paul and now in his eighties he "thanks God for crusts which gave life."

Inevitably, my research has led me to try to find photographs related to the Ciekas' trek and in this search, the internet has been invaluable.

I was fortunate or some would say unfortunate to find harrowing photos which appear in this chapter of refugees with horses, wagons and carts travelling in a long snaking line across snow covered ground, possibly the frozen Frisches Haff. I found pictures of tracks through forests and of Danzig streets also with similar columns of people, wagons and horses.

I have shown these to Paul, hoping to jog his memory. His response was as follows:

"I have looked at the photos and they have evoked good and bad memories. Progress of marching kilometre after kilometre to something better and safer than what we left behind and witnessed on route."

When viewing one of the photos of refugees on a track through a forest with German soldiers walking beside, Paul noted:

"I was puzzled by the two German soldiers who appeared to be escorting refugees. Past life is full of mysteries at times."

My own thoughts are perhaps these soldiers had been told to keep the refugees moving so as to allow military vehicles to pass unhindered or had they deserted but then surely they would have taken off their uniforms. Who knows, it was war!

Regarding the Danzig photo, he commented:

"The Gdansk photo. Of the miles of wagons this was very interesting but also sad and who provided food for the horses?"

With the Ciekas' arrival in Flensburg, it appeared that the worst of their journey from East Prussia was over and hopefully they would benefit from better living conditions, more food and clothing and some stability in a settled location with more permanent accommodation. But as we shall see, their new life in Denmark, still as German refugees, was not going to be as good as perhaps they may have hoped and there were still difficult and challenging times ahead for both mother and son. But before then, they have to get to Denmark.

Chapter 5

Sanctuary in Denmark

After three months of marching, suffering terrible hardships and seeing sights which would horrify any adult, let alone a child, the young Cieka and his mum, had joined thousands of others in the town of Flensburg. However, very frightened, they still had to endure the regular bombings most nights.

Paul recalls:

"We hoped that we could leave Flensburg and be allowed into Denmark for a better life. After all the German military had occupied Denmark, but we soon discovered that our Fuhrer (leader), Herr Adolf Hitler, 'Uncle Adolf', as we were taught as children in school, would not allow any refugees into Denmark."

In the early part of 1945, both the Danish Government and the Interim Government in Germany then estimated that around 300,000 refugees were congregated at the Danish border. These consisted mostly of women, the elderly and children, a third of whom were under the age of 15, including our Paul.

Good News! On 4 February 1945, Adolf Hitler ordered the Danish border to be opened and as a result of this order, 230,000 refugees streamed into Denmark, with the first refugees arriving in Copenhagen on 9th February1945. The refugees were initially housed in schools, sports facilities, warehouses, hotels and private accommodation.

The Refugee Administration was not established by the Ministry of Social Affairs until the Autumn of 1945, problems with normal

Subsequently this led to 1,100 small camps being established. The refugees were then placed in guarded larger camps by the Danish authorities in ex-military quarters, because the Allies had forbidden the refugees returning to Germany. At the time of the German surrender, there were about 550,000 Germans in Denmark which amounted approximately to some 14% of the Danish population. The Danish Census of 15th of August 1946 records that there were 113,997 refugees, including the Ciekas, from East Prussia.

Paul's hopes were eventually realised.as mother and son with forty other mums and children were very fortunate in, April 1945, to be put on board a German minesweeper, by German police. This was after a very severe air raid and the sewage incident. This particular transportation had as its destination, the Danish city of Sonderburg.

It is possible that there might be a further reason for the Ciekas boarding the minesweeper and this may be because any further travelling westwards was blocked by the Soviets or this may be the reason that mother and son boarded a train to take them to Flensburg.

According to Henrik Havrehed's book, 'German Refugees in Denmark 1945-1949', the first weeks of the evacuations from Germany which were by sea and were under winter conditions and often in severe frost conditions could only take place with the help of ice breakers......From January to 5th May 1945 the harbours of Flensborg and Sonderborg were traffic bottlenecks. Sailing took place in minesweeping routes and in convoy with military (naval) protection vessels, albeit danger was ever apparent from Soviet aircraft and submarines.

After the Soviet army's offensive in January 1945, more than two million soldiers and refugees were safely secured across the Baltic Sea from the German ports, and many of them ended up in Denmark. All types of ships were used, for example, warships, troop transport ships, cargo ships, fishing boats, tugs and tankers. But the trip over the sea was not without danger. A Soviet submarine sunk the big passenger ship Wilhelm Gustloff, which was filled with refugees. There is no one who knows exactly how many refugees the ship had, but it was known that approximately 1,239 were saved. Wilhelm Gustloff sank in less than 50 minutes.

This gives us some understanding as to why the Ciekas were put on a vessel such as a minesweeper leaving Germany and the perils they still faced before reaching the relative safety of Denmark.

We are not precisely sure of the date but when the minesweeper actually 'swept' out of the Flensburg harbour into open sea, sorry about the pun. Paul recalls that the weather was very rough. The trip would have taken the refugees east from Flensburg down the fjord of the same name then north to Sonderburg which lies at the southern extremity of the Als Sund. The minesweeper then anchored in the harbour.

Rather than being taken on shore, this German navy vessel became Paul and Lydia's home for the next 4-6 weeks.

"Our first refugee camp in Denmark in 1945," Paul recalls.

Little did he know that it would be the first of many in the next few years of their troubled stay in Denmark.

During much of World War II, Denmark was occupied by Nazi Germany. The occupation began with Operation Weserübung on 9 April 1940, and lasted until German forces withdrew at the end of World War II following their surrender to the Allies on 5 May 1945.

Paul recalls that British soldiers seized the ship on its arrival in Denmark and asked all the German men on board, mostly marines, to raise their left arm for inspection. This was to see if they had the SS mark tattooed there. All the sailors were then taken off to be incarcerated as prisoners of war.

"Actually, the Germans were very glad to see the British, although they were taken prisoner but there were no handcuffs," recalls Paul.

I expect that they preferred the British as their captors rather than the Russians.

The purpose of searching for the SS mark on the German marine's arms was that the SS blood group tattoo was applied, in theory, to all Waffen-SS members. It was a small black ink tattoo located on the underside of the left arm, usually near the armpit. The Waffen SS were to be considered a priority for blood transfusions by German medical staff in the event of serious injury.

It was also thought by the allies that members of the Waffen SS were among the Germans most likely to have committed war crimes; hence the British were keen to identify them for potential prosecution.

Paul can still picture in his mind the marines being taken to the P.O.W camp across the bridge over the harbour at Sonderborg. He remembers waving to them and shouting 'aveidersen.' Although Paul doesn't mention it, the Ciekas must have received good treatment on board the minesweeper.

Before I continue with the Ciekas' journey, some background information relating to how refugees were accommodated in Denmark is essential to aid in understanding what was happening in Denmark at this time.

"With the large number of refugees staying in Denmark during the summer of 1945, the allied forces declared that the refugees had to stay for the time being." (Immigration Museum Farum, Denmark).This meant that they would not leave before the winter as stated by the British. However even if the refugees had to be accommodated, it was crystal clear that the Danish Authorities were very much opposed to any integration of German refugees into the Danish population.

Whilst initially, on their arrival in Sonderborg, the Cieka family were under the administration of the German minority of Sonderjylland (collaborating with the Wehrmacht) and expected soon to be allowed to return to Germany, the situation changed from 5th May 1945.

During the summer of 1945, all refugees were registered to distinguish the different categories to be dispersed among the smaller or larger camps. Camps for German refugees were administered by the National Civil Defense (Statens Civile Luftværn), while camps for allied refugees or displaced persons were administered by the Danish Red Cross (Dansk Røde Kors).

The refugees were housed all over Denmark. The Danish authorities established a separate organisation, Flygtningeadministationen (The Refugee Administration) to look after all aspects of the administration of the refugee camps. The old NCH files I have seen include a number of letters to and from this organisation.

I have also actually seen originals of the Cieka registration cards used after the war in Denmark when I visited the National Archives in Copenhagen, a slice of living history! Although they contained very limited information, they gave me a strong and real connection to 1940s Denmark.

Nationalities were mainly kept together, the Ciekas, as German refugees, were kept separate from Jews and Social Democrats who had fled the Nazi regime and other non-German refugees. The camps which housed the German refugees were administered by Statens Civile Luftvaern (A.R.P-Air Raid Precautions/Civil Defence).

During June 1945, Danish health authorities undertook the vaccination of all German refugees against typhoid, paratyphoid, and dysentery. Risk factors include poor sanitation as is found among poor crowded populations, as probably occurred on the trek and in the refugee camps.

Everybody under 18 years of age was also vaccinated against diphtheria and this is confirmed by the information contained in Paul's NCH Registration document so this evidence must have been available to the NCH in 1948. The photograph of Paul taken from this document provides part of the cover for this book.

This programme of vaccination was later extended to everybody between 18 and 50 years of age. Tests for tuberculosis were also carried out, and all persons with negative results were immunized.

An example of a vaccination card shows that Herman Mack was vaccinated for paratyphoid in June, 1945 and again in 1946 by Statens Seruminstitut, the State Serum Insitute, while he was checked for tuberculosis in October, 1945. I am sure Paul and Lydia would have had such cards for how else would the NCH have known about their medical history?

The Camps were run by Danes with a Danish camp leader. These were either ex-resistance leaders and army or civil defence officers.

However, the daily internal organisation of work, cooking, education, cultural pursuits, camp administration, religious services and many health functions were undertaken by the refugees themselves. Adult refugees were only allowed to work inside the camps. It appears that the refugees had to be guarded which was the responsibility of the Danish Civil Defence. For most camps all these activities took place behind a very strong barbed wire fence which surrounded the camp.

For more information on the composition of the refugee population in Denmark between 1945 in 1949, please refer to Appendix 2 at the end of this book.

At the end of the German occupation of Denmark in May 1945, the German refugees were lodged in schools and sports facilities. The refugees were given access to libraries but only with carefully selected literature. This could have been the start of a process which has been called 'de-Nazification,' or the re-education of Germans by ensuring they read only appropriate books/newspapers.

Signs placed by the Police at the fences of the refugee camps stated: 'Warning. All access to German refugees is prohibited. It is forbidden to stand still or to move back and forth along the refugee camp's fence or in its immediate vicinity. Violation involves criminal liability.'

These were very Draconian measures and I am sure the Ciekas would have been aware of such notices when in the camps and more than likely fully complied with them. What choice did they have? I am sure that they were just glad to have escaped the horrors of warfare in Germany and the threat of capture and possibly worse treatment by the Russians.

It is also worth noting that even within the different groups of refugees themselves there appeared to be different treatment and discrimination. German refuges like the Ciekas were not allowed to leave the camps without special permission, whilst refugees from other countries had more freedom of movement to go out of the camp. Perhaps the Danes still considered Germans to be their enemies?

It is quite ironic that Paul and Lydia were told before leaving East Prussia that changing their name from the Polish sounding Ciecka to Cieka, a more German sounding name would actually improve their chances of survival and yet the Danes seemed to be very wary of the Germans!

Eventually, Paul and Lydia were taken off the minesweeper and marched with an escort into the town of Sonderborg to a modern school in the centre of town, which was to be their next home.

My own research and confirmed by the information from a very helpful Danish contact and expert on refugees, Leif Hansen Neilson, from Denmark, suggests that the Ciekas' first home on mainland Denmark was probably the Sct. Jorgenskolen on the church square. Paul certainly does recall the church square with the church with a very tall spire, so it all seems to make sense.

The Ciekas were actually billeted in the school hall complete with its piano. Paul remembers ropes and rings, a pommel horse and landing mats for 'turnen' or gymnastics. Once inside they found piles of straw on the floor which they used to fill bags and this was to be their bedding, a straw filled mattress. There were lessons in the school but Paul's memory has not stretched to knowledge of the specific subjects so I am unable to report what subjects were taught. Not surprisingly his memory is of PE with simple exercises. He must have enjoyed the physical exercise.

Living in the school, they were joined by other refugees who were all looked after by Danes. By this time the war had ended and there was a Home Guard, a Civil Defence Unit (CDU) in control.

Paul recalls the early days in Sonderborg School. They were not ill-treated but clearly they were considered as enemy refugees. They were in fact German refugees who needed help and care and who had lost their home and most of their possessions.

It seems as if Denmark had previously tried to make sure that the refugees were taken back to Germany under the slogan 'repatriation.' However these negotiations between Denmark and the Allies as occupying powers in Germany were unsuccessful. Thanks though to the Danish freedom fighters against the German occupation, Denmark was recognised by the allies as a victorious victor of the Second World War this meant that the refugees were prisoners of Denmark under the terms of the Geneva Agreement and it may help to explain why the German refugees were kept in the refugee camps behind barbed wire.

The school in Sonderborg was to be their home for their first Christmas in Denmark. It was their second Christmas since leaving Arys. The first had been on the trek which must have been a real ordeal with very little Christmas cheer.

Paul has told me that he doesn't remember how it happened but some kind soul, presumably a local Dane, donated a Tannenbaum (Christmas Tree) with wax candles. This appeared in the school hall where the Christmas Service was held. Small presents began to appear in dribs and drabs such as nuts and fruit. Later Paul discovered these were donated by Danish Christians, probably Lutherans, as this was the national church of Denmark and still is to this day. The Ciekas were also Lutherans.

The continuation of these kind acts depended very much on whether the CDU guard was stationed at the school entrance. Sometimes they would chase the well-meaning Christians away and not allow anything to be left for 'the enemy' i.e. the Germans, even though they were refugees!

Some presents were however safely delivered and went on to be sorted by the Camp Committee and arranged according to the ages of the children. Unfortunately Paul cannot remember the gifts he received at 9 years of age but I am convinced that they would have been well received by the Ciekas.

For some time Paul and Lydia were not allowed to leave the school because, as Paul says, "we were considered to be a part of the Germans who had invaded and who had occupied Denmark."

In time though, they were trusted to go into town and elsewhere. Some of the ex-refugees began to arrange country walks. Paul particularly remembers this change of attitude and the wonderful walks undertaken such as the one they took to Dybbol hill and mill, a few miles west of Sonderborg, to see the war memorial obelisk and windmill.

The obelisk had been erected to the memory of the Scandinavian volunteers of the Slesvig wars in 1848-50 and 1863-64 which were lost to Prussia. I am sure this increased freedom was really appreciated by the Ciekas and all the other refugees.

At the school there were about 100 German refugees including a Roman Catholic father and a Lutheran pastor. But by July/August 1945, there were signs of increasing discontent among the local Danes. For some time it had become clear that Danish shops wouldn't sell their goods to German refugees.

Eventually posters and banners appeared suggesting, in no uncertain terms, that the German refugees should leave after Christmas.

Fearful of a protest against the refugees, because the Danish children were not able to go to their own schools, the refugees were moved out of town to an ex-Luftwaffe early warning station which had been originally established to give warning of incoming allied bombers and their routes.

There was a lot of pressure by Danish parents on the local authorities to give the schools back so that their Danish children could continue their education. It was apparent that from 1945 to 1946, German refugees were generally moved from schools, sports halls, small hotels and small camps to larger camps. However, living conditions in these camps were often poor.

In some of the camps, food rations were extremely scarce and medical care was inadequate. "In 1945 alone, more than 13,000 people died, among them some 7,000 children under the age of five." (Manfred Ertel. 'A Legacy of Dead German Children,' Spiegel Online, 16 May 2005).

The Ciekas experienced the situation at its worst following the German capitulation. It was at this time, when they had just reached Denmark, that Danish hospitals and doctors were reluctant to treat German refugees. This was as a result of anti-German resentment, but also it appeared due to the lack of resources, the time needed to re-build administrative structures and the fear of epidemic diseases which were highly prevalent among the refugees.

The NCH were also worried about this when considering the transfer of German refugee children to England in 1948. So the details of previous diseases and vaccinations received by the children had to appear on the personal details document of all the NCH Children from Central Europe in 1948. Paul's own document indicates that he had suffered from measles, diphtheria and chicken pox and had been immunised against diphtheria later.

Danish Authorities established a camp–internal medical system with German medical personnel, which took time to get off the ground. Paul has told me that the German Red Cross did the medical examinations and immunisation.

"During Autumn 1946, the refugees were divided into about 100 camps. Each refugee had between 2.5 and 3.8 m2 at his or her disposal, besides a joint area of 1.5 m2 per person. Clothes were either donated or bought. For instance in 1947, the refugee administration bought about 200,000 pairs of clogs. The sanitary conditions were problematic. A total of circa.17,000 German refugees died encamped in Denmark.

The refugees were occupied doing practical work in the camps, and workshops were set up with different crafts. A few camps were for instance growing tobacco." (Courtesy of the Immigration Museum, Farum, Denmark).

Generally, in the camps, there was school education to the upper secondary level, work duty for adults, study groups, and theatre. There was music and self-issued German newspapers. The food rations, initially completely inadequate, eventually became more sufficient.

The first camp for the Ciekas was a small one near Dybbol and the refugees were housed in the former barracks. Paul is sure that there were a number of extended static caravans on this camp pulled into position by tractors. He must have watched all this happening fascinated by the manoeuvring.

To try to find out more about the Ciekas time in Sonderburg, I have tried to seek help from the Varde Museum in Denmark.

Unfortunately for my research there are no personal registration cards in existence of the German refugees in the Sønderborg area. So it is not possible to confirm without any doubt which was the school/camp where the Cieka-family were first placed. There appear to be four possibilities: The Alman School (Almanskolen), the gymnasium (Statsskolen), the German private school (Hertug Frederikskolen) and the Sct. Jørgensskolen.

These were all in use as refugee-camps from before the end of the war and till the late summer/autumn 1945.

My contact Leif Hansen Neilson, a well-known Danish authority on German refugees, who has provided some of the following details of particular camps, believes that it was the Sct. Jørgenskolen at the church square. His reasoning is that the only refugee-camp on the Dybbøl side in Sønderborg, as mentioned by Paul, was the so called "Barakkerne ved Aabenraavej" (the huts at Aabenraavej). It was opened as a refugee-camp on the 6th of August, exactly the same day when the last refugee left Sct. Jørgenssskolen. The school started again as school in September. Almanskolen too started as school in September, but the refugees here left the school a bit later, during August, but there is another possibility. The Statsskolen was first free from refugees in October and the Hertug Friedrikskolen in February 1946. (Leif Hansen Neilsen e-mail)

However unfortunately his more official records do not seem to quite tally with those of Paul's memory.

This is because the last refugees were moved from the school which is the most likely of those camps mentioned previously in Sonderburg to Abenraave Aabenraavej" on 6 August 1945 with the school re-opening for Danish children in September. Paul recalls actually spending Christmas at the school which does not seem likely now. The very vivid Christmas memories recalled by Paul may in fact relate to another Camp! All we do know for sure is that the journey from Arys to Flensburg took about eight months so that would place the Ciekas in Denmark around July/August 1945 which seems to tally with them moving out of the school in Sondeborg in late August 1945 possibly.

'Barakkerne ved Aabenraavej' were wooden huts with roofing felt, but with electricity, latrines, stoves and some kitchen facilities. They were about 300 square metres in size. Approximately 110 refugees were placed here in August 1945. In the St. Jørgensskolen there had been 314 refugees (220 adults and 94 children), and at the Alman school 344 German refugees (223 adults and 121 children) and an infirmary with 122 adult patients/refugees.

In total there were around 6750 refugees in the Sønderborg area (Sønderborg police district) in May 1945. Half of them were in camps, the other half accommodated in private homes, primarily by the German minority. Throughout the summer and autumn of 1945, all refugees were placed in camps. There were 31 camps in the police district, 13 of them in the town of Sønderborg.

Although the huts at Aabenraavej were well-situated on the beach of Alssund – they were part of the local, German owned shipyard (Schaumanns Værft) – they were not fit for occupation in wintertime, so in January 1946 refugees were moved to Hørup Klint, - the largest camp in the county of Sønderborg. In the spring/summer of 1946, when the camp was at its largest, there were 1375 refugees in Hørup Klint. Please see below.

Information, maps and photos below are by kind courtesy of Institut for Sønderjysk Lokalhistorie with details of the contacts very kindly provided by Leif Hansen Neilson.

For more details of how I established contact with a number of Danes who were extremely helpful with my research into the Ciekas' time in Denmark, please refer to the chapter later in the book when I describe in detail my visit to Copenhagen on the trail of Lydia and Paul Cieka.

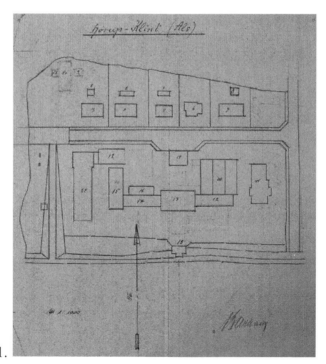

1.

Source for the map above: Compensation Cases, County of Aabenraa-Sonderburg, More Packages. In: Landssarkivet for Sonderjylland.

Map from January 1944 which was used in the calculation of compensation for owners A / S Hørup Klint in 1949 (14). Most buildings are from the original torpedo station before WW1.

1 a and 1 b: Sheds, 2: septic 3: Horse stables and garage with apartment on the 1st floor (brick / tiles), 4, 5 and 7: 3 two-family houses (brick / tiles), 6: Single Family (brick / tile) 8: 3 outbuildings with laundry and fuel space (brick), 9: wooden shed, 11: Former administration building that served as a field hospital in the refugee camp time, 12: Factory building, 13: Workshop building, 14: boiler house, 15: compressor, 16: Forge, 17: Warehouse, 18: Lift Building originally used to bring down the torpedoes to the bridge. Later refugees were living in the building, 19: Water Tower, 20: Trælagerbygning in the refugee camp period was used for lodging, dining hall and school (listed from north to south), 24: Residential Barak.

At each camp, the Ciekas had to be registered and some of their Cards are in Appendix 4.

This was not to be the Ciekas home for very long as soon after they were moved again, probably in January 1946, to their third refugee camp. This in fact was the same Horuptklint mentioned above, a much larger, ex-Luftwaffe early warning station, (see photo on page 69 and map1 above, which had a large military hospital. There were a number of single storey wooden barrack buildings on this camp.

(Source; Peter A. Christensen(1986):

A report on Horup Klint. 1 : Annual Report for Local History Society for Horup.)

"Shortly after the war in May 1945, the research station on Hørup Klint became a refugee camp. At Hørup Klint, systems were developed that could interfere with allied bombers radar navigation systems and systems that could prevent enemy tracing of the German submarines.

The refugee camp was one of the largest in Southern Jutland and by far the biggest in Sønderborg Police District with over a 1,000 refugees." (Source: Compensation cases etc.).

According to records from Statens Civile Luftvaerns, the camp housed 1,266 people by 1 October 1946 whilst the attached refugee hospital had 109 patients. This refugee camp existed longer than most others in the police district and was in use until 1 October 1947. Several of the other smaller camps were continuously closed and the refugees transferred to Hørup Klint.

Map 2 is of the refugee camp but both the origin and year are unknown. The entrance to the camp was far to the right to the north. The first building was the guard room and the next was the administration barrack

Together with the barrack block which housed the guardians of the camp there was also an administrations unit where the Chief Executive, Jes Jørgensen, such a grand title, had his office with one or two helpers. As it was such a large refugee camp there was a great deal of administrative work to be done, hence the need for more clerical staff.

In terms of how the camp was organised, the refugees were guarded by British soldiers, then by Danes in the guise of civil protection people (CB'ere) and finally by Danish marines.

(Source: Anne Marie Bladt Petersen (2000): My time in Horuphav as a child and a young girl.1: Annual History of Local History Association for Horup Sogn).

The Gasworks manager of the Sonderborg Gasworks, Munch Jørgensen, was the head of the camp but he was conspicuous by his absence. He must have been busy elsewhere perhaps doing other perhaps more important jobs, who knows?

2.

"View of the south over the barracks in the eastern part of the refugee camp seen from the watch tower where a small light bulb is placed. The picture is from the post-war era where the camp was guarded by Danish soldiers. The light bulb is not the big light bulb that was set during the war. The light bulb on the picture is probably set up after the war for the guarding of refugees. The barrack to the left was the administration barrack where the daily leader Jes Jørgensen had an office." (Source: Peter A. Christensen (1986) etc)

As I have said, the Chief Executive was Jes Jørgensen who often went fishing and once rode his bike into the sea at Høruphav. Reportedly he was considered excellent for the management task, that is running the camp, but it would appear not a particularly proficient cyclist! We don't know if he was an expert at fishing or just an enthusiastic amateur.

As far as we know, he was calm, even tempered and with much common sense. He did much to facilitate the lives of the refugees in the camp. Jes was able to borrow horses and farm machinery from Skive Farm, nearby, so the refugees could cultivate vegetable gardens in the camp, kokkenhaver in Danish, so providing a good supply of vegetables and much added nutrition to the residents which wasn't always the case in the refugee camps. So it seems as if not all the Danes were anti-German. This very colourful description of Jes also comes courtesy of Peter A Christensen.

The living conditions for the refugees initially were very basic to say the least but gradually improved. For instance there was no running water or toilets in the residential barracks. Residents had to use common washing and toilet facilities. Toilet contents were collected and discharged in a molded container. - This plant was called a Schaffhausen .

At this camp there were two types of barracks. The most common had an entrance to a small room which was in the middle of the straight corridor. From this room there was access to two large living areas - one in each half of the barrack. The second type of barracks consisted of a single very large space in addition to a small hallway at the entrance door. The refugees made their own Cabin carpets. But there was little room for much privacy.

As with British and American POW camps during the Second World War, several of the barracks had names, such as Stalag number 12 as in the British war films. At Horupklint, one was called the Virgins Chamber, another Amazon Temple and a third was called Stalactite cave. Perhaps it is best to merely speculate in private the reasons for these names. I am sure most readers can guess!

There was hospital radio in all the barracks so that messages could be sent to the residents from administrationsbarakken, the administration barracks.

Most of the time, however, the radio played taped German 'desire concerts.' I haven't been able to find out what these were. In the camp there was also a cinema and library. The refugees had different backgrounds and abilities. There were also tailoring and shoemaking workshops and a volunteer fire brigade that consisted mostly of 16-17-year boys. Perhaps Lydia with her family background in tailoring could have helped.

The Fire protection service, an essential requirement with all the wooden accommodation blocks, possessed an excellent motor spray which they used to good effect to put out a fire outside a camp in Mintebjerg.

It is reported that the refugees came from all walks of life, from the poorest to the finest. There was even a German baroness with her entourage of servants. Opposite the hospital there was a small mortuary. Most of the people who died in the camp were subsequently buried at Hørup Cemetery. After 1965, the dead were exhumed and moved to the big graveyard for refugees at Oksbøllejre.

This description has kindly been provided by Peter A Christensen.

According to Anton Marckmann (2006), as early as May 30, 1945, there were 468 refugees in the camp. This figure rose steadily up to 7 February 1946 when the camp accommodated 984 refugees. Some of the refugees came from the German tourist ship Oceana which was laid up for a time in Hørup Sea so that the refugees could get ashore.

It seems as if the Danish Refugee Administration wanted to positively market this camp, perhaps like the Butlins or Pontins holiday camps used to do in the UK in the 1950s and 1960s!

This is how Officials from the Danish Refugee administration (Flygtningeadministrationen) described Hørup Klint when they first visited the camp in December 1945:"

"On one of the most beautiful places in Denmark, near Høruphav, with view to Kegnæs and the Baltic."

The Germans had in fact established, in 1906, a torpedo testing centre with administration buildings, garages and homes for the staff. After North Schleswig in 1920 was reunited with the rest of Denmark, the place was used as a residence for homeless people. But, following the German occupation, the German army once again took over and converted it to a direction finding station [to locate allied flyers]. At the same time several huts were erected for the staff.

"Here in these buildings they have established a large and a fine camp with a lot of good solutions. It will, when it is completed, be one of the best, and for sure the best situated, camp in Denmark." (Flygtningeadministrationen)

Despite this glowing description, almost too good to be true and it was, there were many problems with the refuse and the sewers, which caused great problems with rats and consequently much dissatisfaction with the conditions. There were 26 cases of typhoid fever in 1945, with seven fatal.

In addition, through the winter of 1945/1946, a lot of new huts were built to take more refugees but from the small camps and from private accommodation. However these huts, such was the shortage of accommodation, were often occupied before they were finished. For example, drainage was inadequate and there was no water in the taps and damp or leaky floors. The camp was closed in August 1947, and the refugees were sent to other – even larger – camps such as Grove Gedhus with 15,000 refugees.

During their time in Denmark, mother and son continued to be moved from place to place, seemingly always in transit, living a nomadic life style. It must have been very difficult, making friends and then being forced to move on again. It's no wonder that Paul was attracted by the stability of a new life in the UK when such a opportunity came his way in 1948 courtesy of the NCH as we shall see later on.

At each of the camps, lights out was at 22.00 hours. There was a long list of strict rules which governed seemingly the every move of the German refugees and these were strictly adhered to by the residents of the camps and strongly imposed by the Danes.

A fellow refugee describes the conditions which I am sure that the Ciekas would recognise and be familiar with:

Charlotte Lutterberg a previous resident of East Prussia, like the Ciekas, stayed in the camp as a refugee for most of her camp life from May 1945 to April 1947.(Source: Charlotte Lutterberg (1989)- ' My Stay in Refugee Camp Horup Klint From May 1945 to April 1947.' Located in Local History Association for Horup Sogn.)

She says that the refugees in the barracks, at the beginning, slept on straw on the floors. Later they slept three to a bed where they slept on straw bags with a blanket over them. It can't have been very comfortable.

In the beginning, there were about 500 refugees but later when several more barracks were erected, the total rose to about 2,000.

The food was made in the so-called camp kitchen and consisted generally of herbal tea for breakfast and a stew for dinner. In addition, every other day the refugees received bread, margarine, sausage and cheese.

There were two doctors in the camp and some nurses among the refugees who also treated the sick. Furthermore, there was both an Evangelical and a Catholic priest who held worship services in the dining room and assembly room. Some of the refugees also set up a sewing room, a voluntary fire brigade and there was education for the children who were taught by teachers and students among the refugees. The camp residents made their own entertainment, there was an opera singer and another refugee organized a carnival. These people, despite the hardships, were very resilient.

Charlotte Lutterberg also confirmed that, in her second year in the camp along with a colleague, she opened a dental clinic with the equipment courtesy of the military. In addition to the camp population, they treated the refugees from a further seven camps in the region as well as the Danish security staff in the camp. As a reward, they were allowed to leave the camp and gain extra food rations.

In the first summer, there was an outbreak of typhoid and many refugees were ill. There were shortages of essential supplies, with no toilet paper and no change of clothes. There were a number of deaths. Later, the worst cases were transferred to Danish hospitals and refugees were vaccinated. This may have been the time when Paul and Lydia were both vaccinated.

In the beginning, there were often raids in the camp by officials. Many of the cherished things the refugees had saved or had brought with them from Germany were taken from them such as pens, cameras and money. Therefore, refugees took to burying these treasures in the vicinity of the camp.

As it happened, the next place the Ciekas were taken was the Grove-Gednus camp near the town of Karup, in central Jutland. This was to be their last refugee camp. Records from the Statens Civile Luftvaern indicate that by 1 June 1946 there were 11,733 refugees in this camp. This camp did eventually house up to 15,000 refugees.

Later to become a NATO base, this camp had many barrack rooms. There were bunk beds for men, women and children and cots for babies. On one day before he left for school, Paul distinctly recalls the following statement from Lydia:

"When you come home from school tonight, I will have a very special present for you."

He recalls also a recently arrived cot in the bedroom. But he didn't think to ask who it was for.

Paul's brother, Hans Peter, he now likes to be known just as Peter, was born in the three storey Horupt Klint Refugee Maternity hospital building on 26 April 1946. This was the nearest hospital to the Gedhus-Grove camp. Paul was now ten years old.

In 2017, now, at over 81 years of age, he clearly remembered that the new baby was provided with a pram by the Danish Christian churches.

This former air base was constructed during the German Occupation in 1940 under the name "Einsatzhafen Grove" (later Flieger-Horst Grove) to facilitate offensive operations against England. Later in the war, it became a base for defensive fighter planes.

Following the British advance into Denmark in May 1945, during which the airfield was surrendered to Captain Eric Brown RN, of the Royal Aircraft Establishment (RAE), a group of nine Ar 234B reconnaissance bombers were found at the base and subsequently transferred by Brown and his colleagues to Farnborough. By December 1945, the air base was taken over by the Danish Civil Air Defence, using it as a refugee camp for 22,000 German refugees.

Control over the area was transferred to the Royal Danish Army in January 1946, continuing the use as refugee camp until 1949. In 1947 the Danish Army Air Corps established a flying school, maintenance centre and logistics office at Karup, preparing for Meteor, Oxford and Spitfire fighter planes. When the Royal Danish Air Force was established in 1950 the area was named Air Base Karup.

It was now at this camp that Paul says that he experienced school life again as from 1946 to 1948 he encountered formal education again. It was here also that Paul made some really good friends.

However, it was clear that living conditions in the camp were tough. Other writers have done extensive research on this topic and described the conditions in the camp as horrible with lots of overcrowding and I do not propose to make further judgements about how the German refugees were treated by the Danish Authorities. It was cold as well although some people managed to purloin wood for the stoves.

What is without doubt is that many children did not survive the camps and one day Paul was asked if he knew that his friends, Gisela, Siegfried and Mannfried had died. We don't know the cause of death but I suspect it was due to disease. He did not know but he must have been very upset! This was very very sad news!

To quote Administration: Kulturhuset Stavnsholtvej- "Many young children died of gastro-intestinal inflammation or undernutrition and malnutrition caused by chaotic housing conditions, poor nutrition, poor toilet facilities and fatigue after a hard exodus to Denmark."

There was strong discipline at this camp and the enforcers were the women with rules enforced with a stick if necessary. I have seen a list of 31 rules and regulations from the Danish Work and Social Ministry, Copenhagen, for purely German refugees, dated July 1945 for Grove Camp. The word 'verboten' or forbidden appears in a number of the rules. The camp was full of families of German military personnel and elderly people who had been on the trek from East Prussia. In fact although the camp was in Denmark and Danes worked there, Paul recalls that it was run by Germans and some were even allowed to work on the administration of the camp.

Paul's recollections of Grove:

"I remember the camp school. Also we lived in a single storey wooden building, divided into three living areas. The building had a front door reached by climbing up steps. There was a corridor inside the building with three doors off it. I had to knock on our door to gain entry to our rooms."

Paul spent 5/6 days attending the camp school but he was not all that keen to be there. As always Lydia persuaded Paul to continue his studies:

"You must go because of what you have missed."

"In total approximately 50,000 children received education in special schools set up in the camps….. Amongst the refugees, 2,000 were selected as teachers. Most important in the selection was that they did not have a past as a Nazi because education was also part of a 'de-nazifying' of the children, who, amongst other things, should learn about democracy." (Administration: Kulturhuset Stavnsholtvej)

Unfortunately some people had to vacate their rooms with the whole building to be used as a school. Lack of proper toilets meant that use had to be made of nearby hedges, can you imagine that? Some of the huts had no lighting for the evening and so it was necessary to go to bed early each night.

The likelihood that Paul could contribute to his own and other children's de-nazification was a very important consideration for the NCH in selecting Paul for immigration to the UK as the re-education of German children was a very important factor.

Paul continues talking about Grove:

"There were some permanent buildings including a camp kitchen. We queued for our food and took it back to the barracks. I remember the lack of cutlery as we picked the meat out by hand, although we did have a spoon."

Although times were tough in the camps, Paul remembers, the church services with fondness.

"A Catholic father took a Protestant service.". I suppose needs must in uncertain times.

"The service was basic with no candles, no altar and no incense. It was more of an ecumenical type service." But it was something to look forward to in these dark days with no knowing what the future might hold for the Ciekas.

"There was also an elderly man who played a squeeze box and there was joyous community singing."

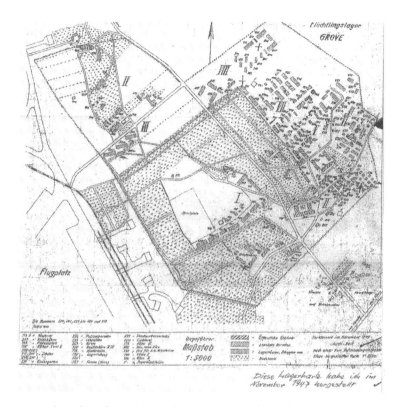

This is Paul and Lydia's last refugee camp before they went their separate ways, Paul to the UK and Lydia with Hans Peter to Germany. Their Barrack, number 415 is described by Paul is lying in "the cluster surrounded by woodland and the arrow indicates." The map is reproduced by kind permission of Flughafenmuseum, Gedhusvagten.

Of necessity, such services took place in converted barrack buildings, with conversions, which the refugees decorated themselves, to principally Evangelical Lutheran, as in Arys or Catholic chapels, because there were no churches available to the refugees.

This was because the German refugees were forbidden from attending Danish churches and this policy was tightened by camp commanders before Christmas 1945. This was because many refugees had wanted to attend a real Christmas carol service in a real church.

It seems that each day in Grove camp had a pattern to it; there was some sort of structure which appeared to be rigidly enforced. This may have been quite welcome to the Ciekas after the very haphazard nature of their journey to Denmark from East Prussia. The day went like this.

At 7 am the small bell in the camp church was rung indicating that it is time for people to get up out of their beds. At 8 o'clock, the female teacher arrived to meet the children and to begin the school. At 12 noon the siren went off for people to set their watches and their clocks that is if they happen to have one.

Letters from Frau Lampracht and Frau Knoblauch provide some information about the details of the accommodation in Grove camp:

"Arno Zilian has carried out adaption work on Barracks 524 in District 5 in Grove camp. The floor area was approximately 10 x 20 metres. Three external doors were fitted leading to 3 self-contained areas. In each room is a stove, two long tables, for long bench seats, a box for firewood, a 40 W lamp and 10 bunk beds. In each of these rooms live seven women, three men, six girls and five boys. The open – air toilet facilities were 300 metres distance. Before winter arrived some of the men had excavated and installed a three-seater toilet close to the barbed wire surrounding the camp. This was used by all inhabitants of the barracks in close proximity, men and women together at the same time."

It seems that Hans Peter's arrival was a bit of a shock for Paul. For years he had been the number 1 son on his mother's list and well looked after but now he wasn't as Lydia's focus naturally enough was on Hans Peter.

Paul is sure that Hans Peter's birth certificate, which was issued by the camp authorities, did bear his father's name. This is of course a delicate subject to write about. However, it appears that it was not uncommon for German women refugees and Danish men, especially security personnel, to enter into relationships.

Paul tells the tale that some of the German refugees were allowed to work on the administration of the camp. In particular there was one person who used to bring treats to Paul and Lydia including cream cakes. Could this have been the father of Hans Peter?

Paul's brother, now with the name of just Peter, has subsequently provided Paul and later me with a copy of his birth certificate. This document does record the date of birth, 26th April 1946 and the time of birth, 7.30 am and the mother's surname, (interestingly Ciecka is used). It noted that the baby was released on the day of birth presumably to return to the camp with mother. It also records the date and place of birth and the midwife, Frau J Gorski who delivered the baby and who it is stated came from Werneuchen near Berlin. We are not sure what she was doing in a Danish Refugee Hospital. There was also a chief doctor or physician's signature who certified with accuracy the baby and mother's name, and both their dates of birth. Interestingly it appears that Lydia's date of birth may have been wrongly scribed initially and then was altered. It seems that there were one or two refugee doctors at the hospital

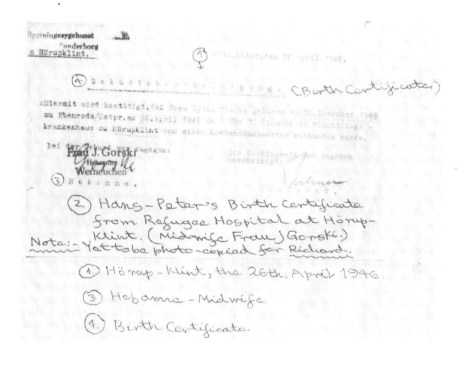

Please see above on this page.

But no father's name is recorded. How time plays tricks with one's memory! Sometimes memory is about what we want to remember!

As I have talked to Paul about the last refugee camp, it's quite strange that Paul's memory is crystal clear about lots of things but particularly on one important matter. This is the location of the latrines, some distance from their accommodation block. When times are hard, it is the basic things of life which assume such an importance.

But for now, I am going to focus on Paul's dad. Whilst mother and son were fleeing both Arys and the Soviet Army, trekking through East Prussia, in very severe winter conditions and eventually arriving in Denmark, but then having to suffer the only slightly better conditions of life in refugee camps, Paul's dad was away still on active service in the Germany army.

The next chapter tries its best to find out what he was doing and as we shall see, he did have a role to play, even though not with the rest of his family, in Paul's future, but not in a way that you might suspect!

Chapter 6

What had happened to Paul Cieka Senior?

You may, like me, are probably wondering what had happened to Paul Cieka senior whilst mother and son were fleeing from the Red Army and trekking across East Prussia and on to Denmark and then being sent from refugee camp to refugee camp. I began to puzzle as to where Paul's dad was all this time. I wanted to try and find out if I possibly could.

But I did recall what that very helpful lady at the museum in Farum in Demark had said. That a lot of German records had been lost or destroyed before or at the end of the war. I really hoped that Paul senior's records were not amongst those. But I did know that Germans, or at least those in charge of prisoner of war camps, when the game was up i.e. the Allies were but a short distance away, had decided to destroy all records. Lots of war films show German soldiers hastily throwing papers on fires before departing. I knew this had happened at Colditz Castle which I visited in May 2018, but would this have applied to German army records in general? I didn't know.

What I thought I knew from Paul was that dad had been a Captain in the Pay Corps of the Germany army, the Wehrmacht, but as to the details of his Service Record, particularly during the war, as is often said "we know nothing."

From the records held by the NCH, I had discovered that he was described as a non-combatant but we all know how unreliable old records can be. Paul's registration document, as one of the ' Children from Central Europe

1948,'with the NCH, states that his father's age was 45 in 1948 when I know from his family tree records that he was born in 1908 so that would make him 40 in 1948 not 45. Similarly, Lydia was born in 1910 so she would have been 38 not 39 as stated in the records.

Trying to track down his service record proved to be quite challenging and the addresses given to us by the German embassy in London, to which Paul did send a of number letters, to find out about Papa, has led us nowhere! What we did have, however, is an excellent photograph of Paul's dad in the uniform of a German officer in the Wehrmacht, the German army. I thought that perhaps I could contact the Imperial War Museum in London to see if they had an expert on German Army uniforms, from World War 2. But unfortuntely, it appears that they do not have the resources to carry out individual pieces of research. Another cul-de-sac!

Paul seems to recall, perhaps from talking to his father after the war, that his dad served at Stalingrad, Russia and also in Norway and was a British prisoner of war at some stage, without any details. But as I have said it has been very difficult to find out anything about Paul senior's war record or indeed his service record.

We are not sure when Paul senior began his military service but we do know that when Hitler reintroduced general conscription in Germany in 1935, the greatest possible care was taken to create a strong military force without disrupting the economic life of the nation.

Men accepted for active service were called to the colours by individual letter rather than by public announcement.

This system was continued in the gradual mobilization which preceded the outbreak of the war in such a way that the wartime Army could be built up organically and the normal course of life not be seriously upset. We don't know what effect Paul joining up had on the family business of tailoring, possibly it was not regarded as a reserved occupation or may be the pay was better in the army or perhaps the life in the army was more exciting. I suspect it was on a number of counts that he was keen to join up.

So that we can try to understand the importance and nature of Paul senior's role in the Wehrmacht, I now provide some background on the system of pay for soldiers which I hope will be helpful to those like me who have no knowledge of such matters.

Every member of the German Armed forces who was on active war time service received tax-free war service pay (Wehrsold), paid to him in advance at monthly or shorter intervals of not less than ten days by his unit paymaster. If he had dependents, wife and son in our case, he would have also received (also when absent as a prisoner of war), family support payable direct to his dependents by the civilian authorities.

All soldiers in ranks from general to private also received a daily combat area service compensation (Frontzulage). This was granted not because of the danger to life and limb but for the "more difficult living conditions" that were encountered. On trips taken in the line of duty, the soldier, regardless of rank, received an allowance for overnight quarters. Every member of the Armed Forces was entitled to free rations, quarters, and clothing; those who had, or were allowed, to take their meals outside also received ration money.

No additional allowance was paid for living quarters in view of the fact that this was already included in the regular pay, whereas soldiers who received only war service pay were entitled to civilian family support. Clothing was free except for officers who received a one-time clothing allowance and a monthly upkeep allowance. Soldiers contracting for professional service received a cash bonus, known as Kapitzrlalztc~rhandgrld. But now back to trying to find out about Paul's dad.

So eventually my continued research led me to the German Federal Archives and the Department of Military Archives and to a Mr Zimmermann. Unfortunately, I drew a blank here again as there were no records relating to Paul Senior, either in the name of Cieka or Ciecka. He did however go on to explain that he regretted being unable to give a positive answer. As I suspected, he confirmed that this was on account of the loss of many written records due to the war and the lack of information on individual soldiers. He did however provide me with another possible source of information, Deutsche Dienststelle (WASt) or German Office in Berlin.

This office was duly contacted with a letter requesting information which had to be signed by Paul. I remained optimistic. I provide this information for anyone else in the future should they wish to do research into the service record of a German soldier in the hope that they may avoid the pitfalls that I fell into.

Eureka, eventually I did receive a reply from a Frau Hildebrand. I imagined her to be very similar to the headmistress, Miss Trunchbull in Matilda, the famous book written by Roald Dahl and of the west end musical fame. This was because of her assertive e-mails but I could be doing her a major disservice as she was probably pretty and petit but I couldn't get the other person out of my head! More of her later as I did have to wait some time for a reply!

But as they say, when one door closes another opens and so it seems this was the case with the research into Paul senior's army service record.

What I mean by this, is that during a trip to Berlin, to Colditz Castle, and Stalag Luft III prisoner of war camp, near Zagan in Poland in June 2018, when visiting the site of the 'Great Escape,' I found a very helpful Polish curator in the museum there. I had decided to take the photograph of Paul senior in his army uniform on this trip. As it turned out I was so pleased that I had taken the photo, just in case.

The curator of the museum, a young Polish chap, called Mirek was very helpful when it came to me showing him the photograph. I think it made his day! It was something different for him to investigate.

He was very knowledgeable about Paul senior's officer uniform and when he was unsure about the details I sought, he was more than happy to do further research there and then on his computer while I stood and watched. It was like having your own personal researcher at your disposal. Fantastic!

I was very fortunate that, on the day we visited the museum, it was very quiet, indeed there was no one else there! Incredibly, a lady had been there earlier whose dad and uncle had been prisoners of war actually at POW camp Stalag Luft III. Although they were not involved in the Great Escape, it was still amazing to think they had been at the same place that we were now visiting. I would have liked to have talked to her but apparently she didn't stay long!

Anyway back to the uniform.

From the photograph on page 86 of Paul's dad, the reader will appreciate that I was really keen to know what the different symbols meant and the colour of them. After all, the photograph was in black and white so it was difficult to tell, just like the 'Pot Black 'snooker on TV when it was only in black and white.

Before, I describe this particular uniform, it is worth noting that in the German military, Waffenfarbe (German: "corps colour") is the means by which the armed forces used to distinguish between different corps or troop functions in its armed services. The Waffenfarbe might be the colour of the collar patch, of the piping (coloured edging) around the shoulder boards or shoulder marks and for enlisted ranks of the piping around the collar and the peaked cap.

I was rather surprised to learn, that some of the elements of the uniform were carried over from the First World War onto a Second World War uniform. Amazingly, it seems that Paul's memory unfortunately, bless him, may have been playing tricks on him. In two ways, the information I had received may not have been quite accurate. (I will return to this later) Rather than being a captain in the Pay Corps, the uniform in the photograph, clearly indicates that Paul senior was a lieutenant, but more than that, he was an Ober lieutenant.

Anyway, apparently, in the German Army, this rank of Ober Lieutenant, dates from the early 19th century. Translated as "senior or first lieutenant", the rank is typically bestowed upon commissioned officers after five to six years of active duty service.

With one gold pyramidal star and surprise, surprise, he was in the Medical Corps with a medical crest in silver, the symbol of the hypocratic oath on each of his shoulder straps (schulterklappen). We would know them possibly as epaulettes. It perhaps is not so surprising, as our own Paul's son is a doctor consultant in the NHS and Paul himself actually trained as a nurse in the UK so it must have been in the blood!

Hopefully, I thought if anything comes back from Frau Hildebrand, the service record may help to sort out any possible confusion and I will come to that in a little while. But for the moment back to the uniform.

The colours of the various elements of the uniform, once we know them, bring life to the jacket and peaked cap. As a member of the medical corps, cornflower blue would be a main colour on the edge of the shoulder epaulettes and the stripes on the collar patches (kragenpatte or kragenspiegel) for commissioned officers.

Incidentally, moving forward in time to the Orzysz museum in Poland in May 2019, Lukatz, assistant curator, gave me a lot of help and in fact actually takes part in WW2 re-enactments, dressing up in German uniform and riding a WW2 bike. He also confirmed, when looking at the photograph, that Paul's dad was in the medical corps. So there you have it!

As we, (well Mirek did most of it), further investigated this photograph, presumably from the 1940s, more interesting details came to light. He thought that the photograph was from 1945 or early 1946. We think the jacket would have been a field grey probably. Above the button-down pocket on the left side of the chest, there are three symbols on square badges, one, is principally red, but in the centre it has a black stripe bordered by two thin yellow stripes and this was awarded for service on the Eastern front. This is known as an Eastern Front ribbon bar. This was apparently a medal he was awarded. We don't know what type of service but we do know the details of the medal.

The Eastern Front Medal, Medaille Winterschlacht im Osten 1941/42 in German, was a World War II German military decoration awarded to both German and Axis personnel. It was awarded to those German military personnel and non-combatants, i.e. Paul's dad, who gave selfless service on the German Eastern Front during the winter campaign period of 15 November 1941 to 15 April 1942. It also included female personnel of the German Red Cross. Instituted on 26 May 1942, it was commonly known as the Ostmedaille, East Medal or Russian Front Medal.

Though being a highly esteemed award, the medal was wryly called the Frozen Meat Medal or the 'Order of the Frozen Flesh' or Gefrierfleischorden in German by Heer, Luftwaffe and Waffen-SS personnel to whom it was awarded. This was due to the numerous instances of frostbite suffered by military personnel during the winter campaign.

Personnel of all branches of the service qualified for the badge if they met one of the following requirements: after a minimum of 14 days served in active combat; 30 combat sorties for Luftwaffe members; 60 days of continuous service in a combat zone; being wounded or suffering a "frozen limb", severe enough to warrant the issue of a Wound Badge. I presume Paul's dad qualified under the third category. Or he may have qualified under the paragraph below.

On 20 January 1943, the qualifications for the award changed to include both combatant and non-combatant personnel (including females) in the Wehrmacht plus foreign members of Wehrmacht units; personnel killed or missing in action and civilians working in area factories.

The design of the medal approved for the award was from a contemporary serving soldier, SS-Unterscharführer Ernst Krauit.

The concave front side features a national socialist eagle grasping a swastika with laurel behind. The back says 'WINTERSCHLACHT IM OSTEN 1941/42' ('Winter Battle in the East 1941/42') featuring a crossed sword and branch below the text. There is also a helmet and stick grenade below the medal loop as well as an outer ring finished in a polished silver effect.

The ribbon that accompanied the medal featured a central white-black-white (white for snow, black for the fallen soldiers) stripe with red (for blood) either side. The medal and ribbon were presented in a paper packet with the name of the medal on the front and the maker name on the reverse. The medal was officially decommissioned by Oberkommando der Wehrmacht on 4 September 1944, although decorations with Ostmedaille continued until October 15, 1944.

Like the Iron Cross Second Class, the medal's ribbon was to be worn on the second buttonhole of the uniform tunic. As the war progressed, millions of soldiers received the Iron Cross Second Class and those who had received both awards wore this ribbon in preference to that of the Eastern Front Medal.

According to Mirek, to receive this medal Paul Senior had to spend several months as a soldier on the eastern front and it could have been as part of a team in the medical corps in a military hospital. He had to spend at least 60 days in the east.

Over three million were issued and many more manufactured.

Paul had been keen to tell me that his dad did serve on the Eastern front during the battle for Stalingrad which was from 23rd of August 1942 to 2nd February 1943 and this could well be the case, given the award of the medal to him.

The medal attached to the bottom of the left breast pocket was in fact awarded for physical exercises by the Third Reich. It is known as a WW2 German DRL Sports Badge and it is of bronze, attached to the uniform by a pin.

The original German Sports Badge or Deutschen Reichssportabzeichen was Die-struck, with an oak-leaf circular wreath and the letters DRA (Deutscher Reichs-Ausschuss) in the centre in a cut out design along with a bow at the bottom.

The sports badge was originally introduced in 1913 by the German Olympic Sports Federation as a way to encourage physical training. Originally it was issued in two types or grades, the bronze and the gold. It is still in current usage but the badge is now issued in 3 classes, gold, silver and bronze. The bronze was awarded to males between 18 and 32 years that had the required physical training for 12 months. Apparently, all soldiers were required to win this award.

During inter-war years it could also be given to the peacetime Reichswehr. In 1921 the badge was expanded to also include eligible females. In 1933 a change was made to the DRL badge which altered the design in the central lettering and in 1937 it was changed again to add a swastika.

The DRL Sports Badge was instituted in 1933 as the "Deutshcher Reichsbund fur Leibesubungen", (German National Physical Training Union) (DRL). It was widely awarded to civilians and military who demonstrated proficiency at athletic events. Tests had to be passed annually in order for the badge to be retained.

Starting in 1933 the DRL badge, though still issued, was mostly replaced by the SA Sports Badge which was a sports badge issued by the Nazi Party. Both badges could be earned and/or displayed by a German soldier who qualified.

Now this is where there seems to be a bit of a conflict between my two experts, both Polish nationals and both working in museums, Lukatz in Orzusz and Mirek in Zagan. Mirek's view is above, but Lukatz believes that the medal is likely to have been something else, but I am not sure what and he has now left the museum so we will have to rely on Mirek.

Moving on, the two other squares above the left breast pocket appear to have an aeroplane as a symbol and these are for length of service, the first is the German Long Service award of the Wehrmacht a four years Ribbon bar and the second is a German Long Service award of the Wehrmacht, a twelve years Ribbon war.

The Wehrmacht Long Service Award (German: Wehrmacht-Dienstauszeichnung) was a military service decoration of Nazi Germany issued for satisfactory completion of a number of years in military service. On 16 March, 1936, Adolf Hitler ordered the institution of service awards for the first four classes.

Each branch of the Wehrmacht (army, navy, and air force) maintained their own version of the Long Service Award and the decoration was issued for four years (fourth class), 12 years (third class), 18 years (second class), 25 years (first class), and 40 years (1939 special class). For the army it was a spread-wing eagle.

The four year service medal was of mat silver and on the facing side was the Wehrmacht Eagle and the inscription "Treue Diesnste in der Wehrmacht" (Loyal Service in the Armed Forces). On the reverse was the number 4 in the centre surrounded by oak leaves. The twelve year award was the same design but slightly larger, in gold, with the number "12" replacing on the reverse.

Paul Cieka Senior in his army uniform of the rank of Ober Lieutenant.

The ribbons attached to both medals were blue because of service in the medical corps. Each of the ribbons also would have had an eagle with wings extended standing on a swastika pin badge.

Moving further down the front of the uniform, we reach the second button; of course; the uniform of a very smart German officer is buttoned right up to the neck. Attached to the second button is a ribbon coloured black with two outer white stripes. I was truly astounded to find out that this was the ribbon which is normally attached to an Iron Cross. Before I was able to ask about the award of such a medal, I was told that it could be possible that this particular Iron Cross, second class, may have come from Paul's grandfather as a result of his service in the First World War. I would need to research this if I could. But this could be difficult as according to Mirek thousands were issued. I hadn't realised and thought that it was more prestigious than this. So I decided to pursue this no further other than recognising that this may have belonged to Paul's grandfather, Paul Cieka, from Konigsberg, East Prussia.

Orders, decorations and medals earned by Germans before the Nazi assumption of power continued to be worn as with Paul's father and were incorporated into the prescribed orders of precedence and uniform regulations for the German armed forces and civil organisations in Germany. German decorations of the First World War were by far the most numerous of pre-Nazi era decorations displayed on Nazi uniforms.

Moving back up to the peaked cap or Schirmmutze, all the various elements, were associated with a particular office, from two blue bands encircling the cap, to the cord at the back of the peak, to the wreath above the cord to the circular symbol inside the wreath with a red centre. This latter symbol was also from the German army in the First World War.

There are also two rectangular badges attached to the collar of the uniform with two blue stripes.

Unfortunately, as I've said before, we don't know when Paul senior began his career in the army. But if this photograph was taken after the war in 1945/1946 which seems very likely, then his service of at least 12 years must have begun before 1935.

I have looked at a number of similar uniforms, on the internet, before the super Mirek came to my aid. I noticed that for many of the uniforms which looked similar to that of Paul senior, some had eagles whilst others did not have the eagle on the cap nor on the jacket. Further evidence that the photo given to me by Paul's brother was taken after the war ended in 1945 or 1946 in Western Europe, is provided by the lack of an eagle with a swastika on the cap. Could it be that as dad, according to Paul, was a prisoner of war and that it was the Allies who took these off as a symbol of Nazi oppression? Perhaps his Service Record would provide the answers?

Apparently, it seems that the eagle insignia was worn as national identification. It was the National emblem worn on uniforms, specifically on the right breast of the tunic and on soft headgear -- that was the Hoheitsabzeichen, also called the Wehrmachtadler (armed forces eagle).

While captured German personnel were generally permitted to retain their uniforms insignia, personnel of the SS, especially the Waffen-SS, were stripped of theirs by the time they were interned.

It is possible that certain troops were retained by the Allies in 1945 in the war- torn former frontlines for clearance duties. This included the processing and transfer of the huge number of POWs, administration and labouring duties. In effect, such troops were used as auxiliary forces needed for the immense restoration tasks. While they were still retained on duty, they may have even retained at least side arms, but were required to remove their national emblems.

Another possibility is that straight after capture, German troops were stripped of their insignia of personal items by souvenir-hunting Allied troops. Many times, as German troops were sent to the other areas, their insignia were removed by support troops too. Such an act could have been taken as a snub to a fallen regime. (Thanks to Jeremy Chan off the Axis History Forum web site for this insight).

According to Mirek, after the war, in West Germany, officers could keep their uniforms but the eagle was cut off. In 1954, in West Germany such insignia were regarded as indicative of fascism. So there we are this is a possible explanation for the lack of the eagle on the uniform of Paul Cieka Senior.

So we now have a better idea about at least some of Paul Senior's war time activities from the uniform. More will be revealed from Miss Trunchball, I mean Frau Hildebrand from Berlin!

She did eventually send me some details of dad's service record, not surprisingly in German. Using the wonderful on line translator has provided much information but I needed some help in interpretation so I have used some German students temporarily at school in Crewe, kindly provided by my friend Kathryn Allen.

The first thing to note is that various documents have been lost and the reason given is that all embracing one of "because of the war." So for this reason, a complete order of service is not available. In what information I have, I've also tried to follow Paul senior's order of service in chronological order.

It is clear that the army pass and army record book and Stamrolle personal papers are not present but from the remaining source material from the former Wehrmacht, the following is confirmed.

The home address: of Wife Lydia C., is Arys / Ostpreusen, Kommandanturkaseme. or command barracks. Presumably this records that the family were living on the army garrison camp. It is not possible to discern the date of commencement of service.

On his Identification tag - it was noted as number eight Group Reserve Battalion 23, this may be a Staff Infantry Replacement Battalion and there is an entry, dated September 1939 which has the same information, whereas it is noted on 25 February 1941, he was part of the Army Catering Unit number 506.

Further information is provided by something which is called the rank list of the Wehrmacht officials in the army as that at the first of October 1942, the period when the battle of Stalingrad was being fought.

Depending on the translation, the officer is identified as a Paymaster or Senior Purser, appointed on 1st September 1941 at the age of 33 and is located in Defence area 1 which is Konigsberg and the record notes the commencement of service as from 1st September 1934 when he would have been 26 years old. So it is a lot earlier than I thought.

The next section is a bit difficult to interpret so I include it as a verbatim translation. "By order of 18.08.1944 concerning employment of Wehrmacht officials as active officers in the special military service (career of the administrative service), the Senior Purser, Paul Ciecka, whose peace time place of service would be the Army Provision Office in Osterode, was employed with effect from 01.05.1944 as a Senior or Upper Purser in the special service for the troops, with the date of appointment 15.08.1936."

I must admit that I don't understand all these different dates. To add to the confusion, it would seem that Paul had it right about his dad being in the Pay Corps and his army service record seemed to back that up. However, particular badges/awards on his uniform seemed to indicate that he was in the medical corps, certainly at the end of his army service. The insignia on the epaulettes for the Pay Corps were very different with different colours and comprised a very ornate 'H' with a 'V' on top. It's all a bit of a mystery! Perhaps the uniform comprises details at the time the photograph was taken, who knows?

The next section reports on Paul senior's two instances in hospital as from 20th October 1942 until 20th November 1942. He was in the Reserve Hospital II in Marienbad- with a sickness, illness or disease since the 5th October 1942. Could he have returned from Eastern front with this condition? From 21st November 1942 to 18th December 1942, he was in Reserve Hospital I Marienbad.

This town lies in the present day Czech Republic although in the 1940s it was part of German Sudentenland and was obviously a good place to recuperate; being a major spa town. Paul Senior would also have felt very much at home there as the majority of the population were German-speaking until their expulsion after 1945.

He was subsequently discharged from hospital to be able to serve in a transport/reserve unit in the town of Parchim in northern Germany where there was WW1 POW camp for British prisoners.

This was the last report and even though Paul had thought that his Dad had served time in a British POW camp, there are no records in existence of him being a prisoner of war. All that is recorded is that Paul Cieka, age 37 on 19 January 1946 was registered as being released from a British release office so he must have been captured at some stage! His last troop unit was recorded as the Army Catering Service 628, his last rank as Senior Paymaster and his address for release was in Eutin, Elizabetstrasse 1, a small town in Northern Germany. How he came to be there we don't know. What's more we don't know anything about his time in the medical corps, as that too remains a mystery! Or if he was captured or simply surrendered to the Allies.

This concludes, for the moment, my research on Paul's dad. But now it is over to me again for a personal trip to Denmark to see what I can find out about the Ciekas

Chapter 7

In Search of the Ciekas

In this chapter, as a bit of a lighter interlude, I explain how I have tried in person to uncover more about the Ciekas' time in Denmark in the 1940s.

For anyone who has undertaken some research, possibly as part of an academic qualification or to investigate a father's service record or just to document a family history, the path taken can be bewildering and exhausting, but it also can be intoxicating, exciting and ultimately very rewarding.

It proved to be just like this as I embarked on a journey back into history with my companions Lydia, Paul and Hans Peter Cieka.

I have tried to describe what life would have been like for the Ciekas in a strange country in the 1940s and one that had previously been overrun by Nazi Germany. It is perhaps not surprising that the population of Denmark at that time may not all have gone out of their way particularly to welcome, with open arms, the large numbers of German refugees coming across the border. Some would say quite the reverse!

As one Dane put it –"first it was the army of Nazi Germany who invaded our country and occupied it, now it's another invasion of the Germans but refugees this time, can Denmark cope?" (Source: Unknown)

As I pondered all those years ago the time the Ciekas, initially mother and Paul, but then later Hans Peter as well, spent in Denmark in various refugee camps, I thought surely there must be some documentation relating to the Ciekas, produced and then later retained by the Danish Authorities.

I knew that throughout history, Denmark had experienced a number of different waves of immigrants and there were actually a number of museums devoted to immigration. Excellent I thought, surely the Ciekas must have been registered as they were moved from camp to camp and hopefully this would be documented and records would be available perhaps in Danish or German.

After some 'too-ing and fro-ing' via e-mail between myself and a couple of museums, frustration started to kick in, I established that the information relating to German refugees would be kept at the Danish National Archives in Copenhagen or Viborg and it could be available to view on line. This was great news, excitement building!

However, this was not to last as I tried to download information, but, alas, it was all in Danish. Not to worry, I thought, one of my friends Bill Young, has a son, Niall, who, having married a Dane, lives in Denmark and is fluent in Danish. Perhaps he could help?

Contact was duly made with Niall and e-mails received from the Archive sent onto him.

To cut a very long story short, lots and lots of frustration occurred, the information that could be useful was only to be found in Copenhagen but was not available electronically and so could not be sent from Copenhagen to Viborg for Niall to translate for me. This was his nearest museum.

It was now clear that I would have to travel to Copenhagen to inspect the documents at the National Archives. 'I would have to visit the proverbial mountain as it would not come to me.'

But first I had to obtain permission to visit as I was not a Dane and would be a temporary immigrant. Over to Niall again!

After another series of e-mails between Niall, me and the Archives, I was then registered, given a password and had my unique number. They now knew I was coming. Despite a misunderstanding over when the documents would be available for inspection, they had only given me a day's notice of the date, I did receive confirmation via Niall that these documents would remain 'above ground', out of the vault, for some three weeks. Yes, yes, yes, more excitement so I booked the flights and hotel and off I went!

I decided on an early evening flight to Copenhagen, arriving late evening and staying two nights so as to give myself one and half days to do my research. As it turned out I was really glad to have stayed for that second morning.

I had a good flight and was soon in Copenhagen and eventually after a bit of a trek through the terminal, I located the Metro.

Now Niall had told me that most Danes speak very good English so I assumed that me, the Englishman, on foreign territory would have no problem in seeking assistance in buying tickets and finding the right tram to a stop near my hotel.

Please, if the reader would enlighten me. Why is it that when in a foreign city, when I ask for help in locating a national monument or my supposedly very popular and nearby hotel, I am invariably greeted with the following response in usually perfect English? This is "Sorry I am not from here." This is exactly what happened to me, only this time the response was "sorry I am not from Copenhagen."

It is Murphy's Law that I pick the one person out of hundreds nearby that couldn't help me. Why is that?

Undeterred, I tried to use my own initiative in trying to fathom out how I extracted the right ticket for the metro from the machine. I soon realised that I was trying to obtain a ticket from a sort of Copenhagen equivalent of the London Oyster card system which allowed no access to me. Soon I had the correct ticket and was on my way to the district of the city where I hoped to find my hotel.

Heading out of the metro station, (I later realised that there was a much nearer metro station to my hotel but on a different line), my route to my hotel, was confirmed by a melee of local youths and my trusty Baddeker map.

As I consulted my map, on route, a number of very friendly Danes approached me and continued to re-assure me that I was on the right route and that it "wasn't too far". I think I made my first big mistake when using an underpass to cross a very busy dual- carriageway.

I found myself in a maze of high brick buildings. They appeared to be mostly residential and my hotel lay somewhere in their midst. Unfortunately not all the streets featured on my map and surprise, surprise, suddenly there was no-one to ask the way.

As I consulted my map again, an elderly gentleman with a small dog of unknown pedigree, strolled towards me. My next mistake was to show him the position of my hotel on the map and ask him the way.

Again, Murphy's Law struck. Whilst Niall had re-assured me that everyone spoke English in Copenhagen, I had found seemingly the only person in the whole city whose English was limited to say the least. I think he understood what I was saying but just grunted and pointed vaguely to the street I was looking for.

Some thirty minutes later and after two further consultations with locals which led me on wild goose chases, I eventually found a student who located my hotel on google maps, showed my location and pointed to the street I wanted.

The phrase hot and bothered was a most apt description for me but thankfully ten minutes later I was standing outside the Hotel Copenhagen, my refuge for the night. But if you thought my troubles were over, you, like me, were clearly mistaken. The hour was after 11 pm and the hotel was shut!

Mercifully, a quick phone call raised the hotel night duty receptionist who supplied a code both for the back door and the post box on the stairs where I found my room key.

Ah well I thought, a good night's sleep and then I would be fully prepared for anything the Danish National Archives could throw at me.

....

...

It was a bright sunny morning as I set out full of hope and expectation to walk the relatively short distance from the hotel to the Danish National Archives just near the Parliament building.

The old building, which housed the Archives, was entered by an old studded door off a square which had a fountain at its centre where particularly Japanese tourists seem to gather to have a photo taken, with formal gardens on all sides.

I arrived at 10.15 am and joined a short queue hoping to gain access to the Reading Room. The man ahead of me in the queue assured me that I was in the right place. Fingers crossed!

Now you will recall that I had booked to see certain documents, had a password to access the so-called 'Daisy system,' don't ask me, and a unique number and they knew when I was coming!

In view of these previous arrangements, any reasonable person would expect to be fast-tracked though into the Reading Room. Oh no, life is never as simple as that, well not in this case any way! When I reached the front of the queue, the conversation went like this.

"Hello, good morning," I said cheerfully, glad to have made it to the Archives, "here is my passport." This was duly scanned. There must be some very valuable documents in the vault I thought.

"Good morning," said the attendant. "Do you have a number?"

"Yes, here it is, I replied confidently, "I also have all these e-mails which confirm my booking."

No answer.

"Please tap four numbers onto the screen"

"Any numbers?"

"Yes"

I tapped in four random numbers and the attendant seemed satisfied, well at least he looked as if he was.

He clearly was a man of few words. There was some delay whilst the good old 'Daisy, 'the National Archives System, accepted me. Eventually after some minutes, I was given, without explanation, a shiny white plastic card, a bit like a credit card and a bigger laminated card on which was a map of the layout of the Reading Room with desk number 14 highlighted. It must be my desk, I thought!

Great, this is it, I thought, I'm in! Alas no, it was not to be! Before he pressed the button to release the barrier to allow it to rise so I could access the Reading Room, we had the following further conversation.

"What are those documents that you are taking in?" he enquired suspiciously and assertively.

"That's my passport," I replied sarcastically.

"What is that?" He said pointing to my mobile phone.

"That's my mobile phone." He obviously hadn't seen one before; it must have been the smart pretend leather case that fooled him!

What are those documents?"

"Those are copies of the-mails sent by the Archives to me." He ignored my reply.

"What are those?"

"Those are documents that I need for my research." Eventually after this interrogation, he appeared to be satisfied with my explanation.

Eventually, I did agree to put my apple and cap in a locker in the cloakroom just to keep him happy. Was there a Danish version of 'a jobs worth' with a hat and an award? I didn't know, but he must be a prime contender for one!

But now yes, yes, I was in through the barrier into the hallowed portals of the Reading Room. I soon found my reserved desk, number 14 and wondered what to do next. I had been given no explanation by our friend on the reception desk.

Clearly the documents weren't going to come to me as if by magic. Apparently, according to my neighbour, an English speaking university student working for the Archive, I had to go to the desk at the end of the room next to the open steel doors into the vault and ask!

This I did and showed the lady hovering expectantly near the desk my e-mails and unique number and surprise, surprise, I had to fill in another form! Clearly, these Danes weren't going to release their documents without a bit of a fight! Well you could knock me down with a feather, within minutes of me completing the form and handing it in, I was handed the box by the same lady!

Well this is it, I thought, I savoured the moment, and what would I find, after all these years? This is history coming to life in front of me. I gingerly took the lid off the box. It was full of index cards in very good condition, considering their age, and they were in alphabetical order. I searched through and found the Ciekas. There were 4 cards in total and unfortunately not as much information as I expected.. Still what there was did need translating. I refused to be disappointed and reminded myself that when these were filled in all those years ago Paul was a young lad, Hans Peter a baby and Lydia was looking after them both without Paul senior, all in a foreign country. I had a piece of history in my hands from the 1940s. This was amazing and very exciting.

Undeterred by this apparent setback, I had expected more, I decided to approach the person who had given me the box. The outcome was both initially very annoying but later proved to be very exciting.

The conversation went like this:

"Hello, I was wondering if the archive had any more information about these German refugees, there isn't much here, "I announced, proudly showing her the cards.

"Oh, what are you going to do with this information, it is confidential," she said in a very superior voice, looking down her nose at me.

"Pardon, I don't understand, I want to use this information in a book I am writing about German refugees."

"But you can't use this information in a book," she said adamantly.

"I am not going to reproduce these actual cards in a book and in any case, I have the full permission of one of the persons named on these cards to use the information." I was getting into my stride now. I continued.

"You are being very un-cooperative. I have come all the way from England, at my own expense. I have e-mails from you confirming my visit and there is no mention of confidentiality. This is part of Danish history and is a story that deserves to be told."

I think I had won her over and she seemed to be softening to me.

"Ok I will ask my superior," she quickly announced disappearing through the gates into the dark vault. I didn't know how long this would take or when she would return. I imagined a Dickens-like figure in a long coat sat at a high desk looking down over his pince nez as the lady cowered before him, on bended knee with her hands clasped subserviently, making her request.

I retired to my desk number 14, somewhat taken aback, no I was actually flabbergasted at what had transpired.

After about twenty minutes the lady returned to say she had checked her files and there could be another file on German refugees 1939-1945. She would investigate.

I waited at my desk, chatting to my neighbour, a young lad called Rasmus and fellow researcher, explaining my situation to him. He suggested I might like to contact an Assistant professor at the University who may be able to help me. I put this lady's name on my list of contacts to pursue.

Not knowing how long the lady would be delving into the archives, I first went for a drink and then later lunch, hoping for good news on my return.

I quietly returned to my desk, and oh, joy of joys, there were a number of photocopied pages plus copies of the four registration cards. I could hardly believe my eyes and no sooner had I settled down when the lady scuttled across, red of face, to explain that she had found these for me. Well I thought I have copies of the registration cards so I will put them in my book. Please see Appendix 4.

The ones for Hans Peter and Lydia are quite detailed, and are shown below, the one that mentioned Paul, not so, so perhaps his original went with him to the UK or he gave it up to the Danish Authorities. His just has his official number as they all did plus his date and place of birth, current residence as Grove and that he left to go to England on 05/07/1948 on Methodist transport.

For Hans Peter and Lydia, there are brief details on two further cards which record the same information but also that they had departed to Germany on transport on 19/10/1948

For finding this information, the lady was clearly very proud of herself and I was ecstatic. They needed translating which I did subsequently, but who cares, I had more information.

I asked her again if there was any more information and she suggested I approach the research worker at the top desk, another person to deal with.

Well, I don't know if the reader has experienced the cheese counter in a well-known supermarket, in the good old days, where you had to tear off a number from a ticket machine. Well this was the same. Now I come to think of it, our local hospital has the same system, for a blood test.

So off I went, to tear off my ticket with my number on it, only to find that there was a queue to see the researcher. Eventually my turn came and surprise, surprise, the nice young man was none other than the brother of my neighbour at desk 14.

He was very helpful, more cooperation indeed! Once he had grasped the situation and been briefed in Danish, by my now 'best friend.'(the lady of the morning's little hiatus), he gave me a couple of contacts and earnestly pointed me in the direction of the Immigration Museum at Farum. This was apparently forty minutes by "S" train from Copenhagen.

He also searched the baptismal records of Horup Klint for the month and year that Hans Peter was born but no luck, perhaps he wasn't baptised.

By the time of my departure, I think I had exhausted all possible lines of research in the archive and exhausted all the staff too. My departure was accompanied by a big thank you to all in the Archives, with a note taken of all their names even the guy on the security desk who had become quite used to me popping in and out and now raised the barrier as I approached. Tomorrow to Farum!

....
....

The trip on the "S" train was smooth and speedy and after 30 minutes or so I left the train at Farum station, the end of the line. I was full of confidence as I headed out of a nice suburban station expecting to see a local notice board or sign at least pointing to the Immigration Museum.

Alas it was not to be, I thought I was getting used to these disappointments!

I had arrived in what appeared to be a very modern small town centre which was fully pedestrianized with cars and pedestrians sharing the same space but no sign of a museum!

Ah well, I thought I will go and sample the delights of a local, very posh, coffee shop, a konditori in Danish and see if anyone knows of the Museum. Two young shop assistants had never heard of it, Murphy's Law again, but fortunately an elderly lady had heard of it and straightaway in superb English directed me to it.

No more than ten minutes had passed and I was standing at the reception of the Immigration museum, hope and confidence fully restored.

My next conversation with the receptionist went like this.

"Hello, I wonder if you can help me. I am doing some research into the plight of German refugees during World War II who spent the years 1945-1949 in refugee camps in Denmark and wondered if the museum had any information which might assist me."

"I don't think so, we don't really have any information on that subject. But you are welcome to look round our exhibitions; she smiled in a sort of non-committal expression, disappointed that I had not been a more interesting person to deal with.

"Oh," I said, that's a pity because I was told by the National Archives in Copenhagen that this museum was very good and well worth a trip. I even tried to contact one of your researchers, Susanne Jensen, who I was told would be very helpful and left a message on her voicemail. This was yesterday."

"Aaah, I see," said the receptionist, suddenly realising that I might after all be someone interesting to deal with!

"Would it be possible to see her this morning," I asked conscious of the need to maintain what little momentum I had gained with the receptionist.

"I think she is in a meeting," was the deflating response.

"Oh," I countered, trying to sound as disappointed as possible. "I only have a short time before I have to catch my train to the airport for my flight back to the UK."

 I will try and see if she can see you," was the surprising response by the receptionist.
There was then a brief conversation between the receptionist and presumably Susanne Jensen which ended with the deflating comment to me.

"She says she is in a meeting and can't be disturbed."

Oh well, I thought, here I go, nothing ventured nothing gained.

"Can I speak to her please," I almost cried, thinking this is the last throw of the dice.

To cut an even longer story short, I explained desperately in detail, my situation, what I was doing and my limited time in Denmark and would you believe it she came straight out of her meeting to see me there and then! Whilst not able to provide me with much useful information at the time, she was in fact a brilliant source of helpful contacts which have proved really invaluable which have provided lots of information to go in this book as you will have seen earlier in the book under the chapter on refugee camps.

I was very grateful to Susanne, tried to leave a donation, which the museum would not accept and left the museum with a spring in my step, full of the joys of spring, even though it was July!

I left Denmark pleased with what I had achieved, eager to carry on my research at home and to input what I had found out. We now come to the process by which Paul decide to leave Denmark for the UK in 1948 and the role of the family in this decision.

Chapter 8

A New Life in England

"In 1948, 118 children were received in England from Germany and from the Displaced Person's camps in Denmark. This was very successful and the children became 'at home' and settled down in the family of the Branches." (Action for Children web site). Interestingly, the original NCH files that I have read describe the number of children as totalling 120, 86 boys and 34 girls.

I have not been able to establish why Paul in particular was selected to be one of the 11 in the third group of German children or one of the 120. Paul doesn't know and can't remember whether he ever did know. He may not have been told! I can't imagine in the 1940s Denmark, ravished by war, that refugee adults or children had much independence. What we do know is that the National Children's Home (NCH), forerunner of Action for Children, interviewed 2-3000 refugees. The NCH received the 118/120 children from Germany and Denmark during the first seven months of 1948 under a scheme approved by the UK Home Office.

Whilst it is difficult to be certain, the impetus for the scheme certainly seems to lie with the NCH. I certainly found evidence that the NCH hoped to approach the Home Office, so as to obtain funding. There was also great optimism that the venture would appeal to the public and that there should be no difficulty in raising enough funds. In addition, it was thought very likely that members of the RAF would wish to contribute. Why? We don't know. Perhaps it was something to do with the raids of Bomber Command on Germany and the sad loss of life but this is mere speculation on my part.

My inspection of old files at the offices of Action for Children in Watford, Herts, has also not thrown any further light on why Paul specifically was selected.

Instead there appears to be a list of general conditions which had to be met. The preliminary selection of suitable children was to be in accordance with their need and this should be determined by the Ecumenical Refugees Commission.

It was clear that only German speaking children should be considered, as the NCH only wanted to deal with one foreign language, and also only those of Protestant Christian parentage.

In an article produced by the NCH entitled 'A Friendly Invasion,' it is noted that, the scheme approved by the Home Office was subject to the following terms:

"It is understood that the proposal is to select promising children (both boys and girls) who are likely to profit by an education in England, and to return eventually to Germany or Austria where, it is hoped they will help in the re-education of their countrymen. The children will all be young –generally under twelve, though there may be a few not older than fourteen- and will be selected after a medical examination, which will take account both of their physical health and of their mental ability."

Another file confirmed that all the children were to be free from infectious diseases, have no head or body lice, and have been immunised against diphtheria. Paul's NCH Admission document under the title Children from Central Europe 1948 confirms that Paul, although healthy, on admission to the NCH, had previously contracted Measles, Diphtheria and Chicken pox. He had also been immunised against Diphtheria and Vaccinated for TB.

I have a copy of a further document from the Danish Refugee Administration in Copenhagen which certifies that "Paul Cieka, born 26.2.36 has been in Denmark as a refugee and can leave Denmark with the permission of the

Danish Authorities." All children leaving were to have the ignominious misfortune of having a large label on a string around their neck giving all their personal details. This was much like the evacuees in the UK.

For Paul, it all started one day, in the Grove camp, with Lydia asking Paul what he had been doing, implying that he had been 'up to no good.' Paul didn't think he had been doing anything wrong, unless it was playing 'kiss chase' with the girls on the camp as lots of the boys did then. It was certainly a common game in the UK in the 1960s. Paul always seemed to have a lot of friends that were girls!

Now I know why, of the friends he remembers from school a number of them were girls!

Apparently, the reason for the questioning was that the Ciekas had been summoned to a meeting with the Lagerleiter or camp leader/commander and mother was somewhat disgruntled. At the meeting there were to be in attendance representatives of the NCH.

Paul does not recall much of the meeting. There was obviously some discussion about the possibility of Paul going to England but he clearly remembers his mother saying: "You are not going….. if I let you go for 5 years, how do I know you will be alive?"

It must have been a major decision for Lydia, as she had looked after Paul through thick and thin, day and night through an extremely bitter winter, with food shortages, sleeping outside, through bombing raids during the walk across the frozen ice of Frisches Haff and afterwards in numerous refugee camps in Denmark and now she might be losing him.

In fact Paul, now 12, seemed less daunted by the prospect of emigration to England than Lydia. He has said to me that he thought at the time that "life in England had to be better than in any refugee camp."

He has confirmed to me during the course of our many chats and discussions that his decision to go to England was prompted by a desire to be free from an internment camp and once he had left Grove he said that: " it felt great to be free from barbed wire, the rations and all those restrictions."

Lydia, respectful of Paul's views, agreed that a letter should be sent to Paul's father via the International Red Cross to seek his views on the matter. Paul senior was at that time living in Eutin, Holstein and had a temporary address at 42 Mahlstedstrasse. We do not know why he was living there.

This raises an interesting matter of the censorship of the mail in post War Denmark.

Whilst there was strict censorship on mail from Denmark to all foreign countries from May to October 1945, with mail to Germany, Japan and Spain censored until March 1947.

It is likely that the letter to Paul's father, as it went via the International Red Cross, was not censored. The reply actually came with a Refugee Administration stamp as it had been cleared in Copenhagen by the relevant authorities.

Paul senior's address at the time of the correspondence was in Germany and it is worth noting that it was not until 4 April 1946 that refugees were allowed correspondence with Germany. Refugees were not allowed Danish money.

Paul, it appeared, was adamant that he did want to go to England, apparently he "had become fed up with life in a refugee camp." So this was a difficult time for mother and son.

Anyway it was Paul who wrote to Dad and Lydia wrote in the same letter that "your son wants to go to England."

The letter was sent by the NCH via the International Red Cross through Hamburg to Eutin, Holstein.

It appeared also that it was not straightforward for Paul Senior simply to give permission for Paul junior to go to England. No! It was necessary for the military record of Paul Senior to be carefully assessed against the rules of the Geneva Convention. The purpose of such an examination was to determine whether he had committed any kind or war crime and so an interview was necessary. As far as we are aware Paul Senior received a clean bill of health in terms of his war record.

Paul believes that his father had fought at and survived the terrible battles of Stalingrad, he had later been sent on Occupation Duty to Norway but was later captured by the English and became a prisoner of the English. Information held by the NCH on Paul's personal file seems to contradict this and confirms that Paul's father, although "a regular army man was a non-combatant."

Paul seems to recall that Father's response, dated 25 April 1948, to Paul's letter had stated:

"I know the English, please let Paul go."

I have seen the letter however and its contents do not seem to confirm such acceptance of the English by Dad. Although he may personally have had very positive views about the English.

Basically, the permission for Paul to live in England for 5 years was conditional. Paul senior did understand what he was agreeing to, he was in favour of the move provided that Paul was cared for and brought up in the Lutheran tradition. The response actually came from the Refugee Administration in Copenhagen, although the letter has the father's address.

Flygtingeadministrationen was the Refugee Administration, a Government Committee set up as part of the Danish Home Office to deal with the problem of 250,000 refugees who found themselves in Denmark in May 1945. Denmark's population was 3.5 million.

At the end of the war, the Allied powers (USA, Great Britain, USSR and France) did not wish immediately to accept the significant numbers of refugees from Denmark. However even Denmark couldn't support large number of refugees on a permanent basis. This included Lydia Cieka and Hans Peter Cieka, who were returned to Germany in October 1948.

After the end of the Second World War, most of the refugees in Denmark were German. On 24 July 1945, The British occupation force, contrary to Danish expectations, decided that they must stay in Denmark until the situation in Germany had stabilised. They were interned behind barbed wire in refugee camps across the country, until it was possible to send them back to their homeland. "The first refugees were returned to Germany in

November 1946 and the last ones going in February 1949. Only very few stayed in Denmark for good." (Bjørn Pedersen: Tyske flygtninge (German refugees), 2 May 2005, befrielsen1945.dk (in Danish).

There were in fact signs placed at the fences of these camps which I mention again to give a real picture of what life was like in the camps.

They stated:

"Warning. All access to German refugees is prohibited. It is for bidden to stand still or move back and forth along the refugee camp's fence or in it immediate vicinity. Violation involves criminal liability. Police"

After the war, the Danish authorities wanted to send the German refugees back to Germany as soon as possible but the situation in Germany was so chaotic that this was impossible. Furthermore, the majority of the refugees came from areas that, after the war, were in Polish or Russian controlled territory and from which Germans were expelled. In November 1946, the authorities started sending German refugees back to Germany. The last refugees left Denmark in February 1949.

The negotiations about when and where to return the refugees had begun in earnest during 1946. A number of criteria were drawn up to decide to which of the four occupied zones, including Berlin, the refugees would go.. A deciding factor was Angehörigkeit ("where they belonged"), that is, where they had family, property, or other connections. Approximately 116,000 refugees could thus be returned to the appropriate zone, but the remaining 74,000 were declared stateless. To facilitate the return, a number of camps were designated as collection points – for example, in Ålborg, Århus, Rom, Grove-Gedhus, where Paul and Lydia were resident and Oksbøl, Kolding, Skrydstrup Tønder, and Kløvermarken in Copenhagen. These places had housed the largest camps, or they were strategically placed on railway routes to Germany.

So in June 1948, with all the formalities completed and after what must have been a very sorrowful farewell to Mother and Hans Peter, Paul set out by small coach with 19 others from the Grove camp on Jutland, with a stop at Oksbol, to Esjberg to board a ship to Harwich, England. He was accompanied by representatives of the NCH and a group of Danish people.

He was part of the Fourth Wave of 25 youngsters received by the NCH which arrived in Harwich on 8 July 1948.

Paul recalls that he felt guilty leaving loved ones behind. Paul was 12 as he travelled on board a passenger ship to begin a new life in the United Kingdom. NCH records of the journey confirm that the trip took 22 hours and whilst Paul can't remember how much time he was on the ship, he recalls a very rough North Sea and that he was sea sick. This was not an auspicious start to a new life in England!

He arrived in the UK on 8th of July 1948 as part of a party of 25 children all from Danish Camps.

Paul concludes: "After three refugee camps in Denmark, my coming to the UK completely changed my world and made me, for better or worse, the adult I have become. I shall never forget my debt to the NCH, for probably, after my refugee experiences; they have given me the 10 happiest years of my life." This was written sometime in the past.

Lydia and Hans Peter left Denmark on 21 October 1948 and were in fact sent back to Germany. Having arrived in Denmark before the Germans surrendered and spent 3 years in refugee camps, mother and son were returning to occupied Germany and to an unknown future.

In fact only about 15 percent of the German refugees returned to their original home. For most of them the area in which their original home had been located had subsequently been annexed by Russia and Poland and they were required to settle in the remaining parts of Germany. Lydia and Paul's brother chose to settle near Lydia's mother's home

.

Records from the NCH indicate that Paul, at various times during his stay with the NCH, was considered for possible repatriation. As many of the children as possible were also similarly considered in this way. Indeed I have seen different lists of children, with Paul included, which indicate that for each child, either:

Parents temporarily unable to have them home but will probably do so later.

Already returned.

Return unlikely as there was no home or the home conditions were considered to be very unsatisfactory

Insufficient information known about home conditions

The list which stated home conditions were known and eventual return was possible included our own Paul.

For all the children, home conditions were reviewed from time to time as it was anticipated that most if not all would be repatriated.

Interestingly, the same NCH file noted that Paul was a German national, that his date of birth was 26 February 1936 and that he would probably return home in July 1958.

The same file also has a letter undated from Lydia from Westfahlen in Germany which asked if Paul could come home for a holiday and that "this occurred last year and this year." We don't know which years these referred to. There was the possibility that Paul could stay in Germany permanently which is, I am sure what Lydia hoped for.

The file notes that the case of Paul Cieka was still being investigated and for the present he is to remain in England.

We know now that he did visit his parents and Hans Peter in Germany but he was to become a permanent citizen of the UK.

It seems at this stage that it would be appropriate to include a couple of family photographs, one of the two brothers, Paul and Hans Peter and the other of the family Ciekas together, presumably this was in Germany.

I suspect the black and white photo on the next page was taken in 1950s as Paul's dad doesn't look much different to the photo of him in his Wehrmacht uniform. It is the earliest photo of the family that I have in my possession.

Talking of families, I finally managed with my wife, Sue, to travel to Poland and visit the town of Paul's birth and early childhood. This was in May/June

2019 and the next chapter describes our amazing visit, who we met and what we found out.

A very nice photo of Paul who is on the left and Hans Peter on the right.

Above the family Cieka.

Chapter 9

Walking in the Ciekas' Footsteps in Arys

I am sure that, having reached this stage of the book, you will agree with me that the story is an incredible one concerning not just Paul, but also mum Lydia, dad Paul senior and brother Hans Peter. So I suppose it was inevitable, given my sense of adventure and love of history, that at some stage, I would have to travel to the town where Paul spent his early childhood. Of course, I'm talking about Arys, then in East Prussia, Germany, but now lying as it does in modern day Poland. The town now has the name of Orzysz.

Paul has never mentioned returning to the town of his early childhood and I haven't liked to ask. I am sure he has his own reasons and who am I to enquire further? Perhaps I might find out when this book is published. But I just had to complete the story and find out what this place, that I've heard and read so much about, was really like, albeit I would be travelling to Orzysz some 75 years after Paul and Lydia had left in haste, on that very cold and traumatic winter's night in December 1944.

I was sure that so much would have changed but I was optimistic that I might get some semblance of what the town was like in the 1930s and 1940s. I would, I am sure walk in the Cieka family footsteps. Just like my trip to Denmark, this journey would be like stepping back in time. Who knows what I would find out and who I would meet? I knew there was a museum in the town because I had tried unsuccessfully to contact it, so I was hopeful that the staff there would be able to help me. So it was, that, in May 2019, with my wife Sue, my companion and co-adventurer on all my recent trips, I set out to discover the town of Paul's birth and early childhood.

In 1944, Paul and Lydia, had left under their own steam, on foot, with few possessions, whilst my journey on Paul's behalf involved much more sophisticated transport arrangements: Essentially it was by car from home to Liverpool airport; a two and half hours flight to Warsaw, a car rental and a journey of about 170 miles to reach the destination in Orzysz. Compared to the journey undertaken by the Ciekas from East Prussia to Denmark, which took some months, we had travelled so much further in a fraction of the time

I had taken with me a number of old photographs of the town, that is Arys, together with a number of documents relating to the Ciekas which I hoped would help me with
 my research. These have proved very helpful.

Driving into Orzysz, we spotted the town's Tourist Information Centre and as luck would have it, it was actually open. This is where we first came up against the language barrier because the lady behind the counter didn't seem to speak much English or perhaps it was our accent that was the difficulty. Oh how I thought to myself, that we take for granted that wherever we Brits travel in the world, the locals will always speak English. Anyway, undeterred, we managed to obtain a map of the town and surrounding area which proved to be so useful in getting our bearings and comparing my old photographs with the buildings on the ground. As I said to Sue, when we walked round, I was sure that the church at the crossroads was the one that Paul remembered and which was attended by the Ciekas and it was the one on my old photo! A current photo was taken. see page 113.

A modern map of Orzysz is to be found on this page.

As we strolled around the small town, unfortunately there didn't seem to be very many oldish looking buildings. Undeterred, we carried on and found to our delight, on the same side of the road as the church, the town's museum

This was the same museum that I had e-mailed several months ago, but the email must have gone into their spam. We were fortunate again as this too was open and this is where our good fortune reached new heights as the

Curator Katarzyna and her assistant, Lukasz were so helpful. They were delighted to help us and even had an old map of Arys, had information on the town, lots of old postcards and provided a contacts for a Dietrich Peylo, a German, who had compiled a book of old postcards of the town.

In the following pages, I have tried my best to compare pictures of the town of Paul's birth in the 1930s and 1940s and the ones of which the family would be very familiar with those taken by me and Sue during our visit in 2019 in the hope that the reader can step back in time. You will have to judge for yourself whether I have been successful.

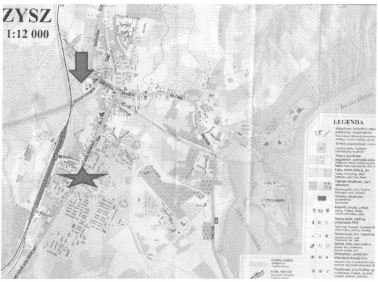

Overleaf, this is a modern map of the town of Orzysz, formerly Arys which was helpful during our visit and was supplied free of charge by the Tourist Information Centre in the town. The layout of the town is similar to that of Paul's day, the scale of the army camp can still be seen,(star) as can the railway, the 'T' junction where Paul's church is sited (arrow)and Arys lake.

There are of course many new buildings in the town which you would expect due to the war and the passage of time since Paul and family Cieka was resident there but I am still able to confirm that the basic layout of the town still remains essentially the same. This is with the centre of the town at the

'T' junction and the bulk of the built development along these roads making up the 'T., although there is some development to the north.

Katarzyna was really pleased to hear about my book and was delighted to photocopy the photos of Paul and his Dad and other historical documents I had brought with me from the UK. So it was a win-win for both the museum and me as I was pleased that I had added to the museum's information base about the town in the 1930s 1940s. As time was moving on, we agreed to return to the museum on the next morning when hopefully more information would come to light. We headed back to our accommodation near Pisz (Johannisburg in German) very pleased with what we had found out so far.

The next day there were more surprises including some information about the population of Arys which provided some evidence of the departure of residents from the town and the garrison camp in 1944 as the red Army continued their push through East Prussia. The following figures speak for themselves:

Date	Population
1939	3553
1947	1102
2018	5615

The town is still quite a small place but it is obvious to me that Arys lost more than a third of its population during WW2 and this may have been due to a biblical type exodus or as a result of the Russian offensive. It is likely the town would have been targeted given the presence of a large military base which would have been a threat to the forces of the oncoming Red Army.

On the next page is the Commandant's house lying within the Camp. Paul has previously recognised it as "the Residence of the Commander of the Camp."

The second photograph on this page is the same building, now outside the confines of the camp in 2019 and with a more simple appearance.

Katarzyna had also managed to find out a contact for the NATO base, the Press Officer, Martyna Kupis for me to ask about the possibility of a visit to see any buildings surviving from WW2, although she was very doubtful because it was a current military base and so it proved. Please see after pictures for more on Martyna.

The Kommandant's residence.

The former Kopmmandant's house is now a Cultural Centre which we were shown round by the Director.

Although I did manage to speak to Martyna on my mobile phone, my request had to be put in writing and unfortunately she needed lots of information about my book and my personal details etc. so this would have to be provided on my return to the UK so no visit was possible but at least I could request photographs of old buildings to be provided, which I did.

Unfortunately, further requests to Martyna later,on my return home ,didn't result in any response, Ah well, I thought, probably the NATO Press Officer has more important tasks to occupy her time such as ensuring the world's media is kept up-to-date with NATO manoeuvres in Eastern Europe. Never mind!

On this page is a significant shop going out of Orzysz, on the main road to Johannisburg, now Pisz and has been recognised by Paul previously as "a big shop" It is still a shop and the 2019 photograph appears below on this page.

From the photograph above it is possible to see how close this shop was to the church attended by the Ciekas. I am sure that Paul with his mum would have bought items from and walked past this shop many times during their time in Arys.

These old buildings are on the camp site and according to Paul were the Officers' restaurant and the Assembly Hall and Rooms.
It was known in German as the Offiziers- Kasino/Kantine. He remembers that between 1940 and 1943, officers' children celebrated Christmas in the Big Hall.

I think that such parties took place at Christmas wherever children were present and dad was serving with the military.

Many of these buildings have now gone and it is not possible to identify the old limits of Markplatz. Paul does, however, remember the four storey white building as a market. It was probably the Buttermarket. It is likely that this Post card dates from about 1942. An earlier same view from 1939 has two ornate gables with finials on the Deutsches Haus.

I believe that this is the same street looking towards the church but obviously much altered from Paul's time and with new buildings, although the building with the triangular pediment, seem to be the same one as in the earlier post card.

On this page is a colour photo of the barracks within the Camp and Paul has "vivid memories of the residencies of the troops in training." I have dated this postcard to August 1909 so possibly Paul may not recall this particular view unless these camp buildings remained until the 1930s.

Paul recalls a picture very similar to the one on this page:

"most clearly because it was guarded day and night and every time we left the Camp or returned we needed to go past the guards." Similarly, this post card is dated as July 1907 but perhaps it didn't change much during the next 25 years or so.

Paul recalls a picture very similar to the one on this page: "most clearly because it was guarded day and night and every time we left the Camp or returned we needed to go past the guards." Similarly, this post card is dated as July 1907 but perhaps it didn't change much during the next 25 years or so.

With respect to the black and white photograph on this page, according to Paul's memory, the first building past the tree on the left in the foreground, was the Post Office and we believe that the smaller white building further down the street on the left hand side was the Lutheran Sunday School.

144

The picture on this page is the 2019 version of the Church that Paul attended with his parents and went to Sunday School from the age of 4 in 1940 until mum and son's departure in the winter of 1944/45.

The photo on the previous page above is from an old postcard mounted on the wall of the museum in Orzysz. Its incorporation in my book is with kind permission of Katarzyna of the museum. I think this is probably much older than the 1930s and 1940s.

It did seem as if a number of buildings from Paul's time in Arys had been destroyed by the advancing Russians and by the post-war Communists, supposedly to rebuild Warsaw after it had been more or less totally obliterated by the Nazis. Many of the materials from destroyed or damaged buildings apparently went missing on the way to Warsaw. We had previously been to Warsaw and visited the Jewish Museum to hear about the utter devastation caused by the Nazis. This was a diabolical act of revenge following the Jewish Uprising and indeed a very, very sad tale.

We continued our walk around Arys and this time the church was open and so we ventured in and took some photos. We had met the priest for this and the Catholic Church further down the road to Elcka. Although not speaking English but only really Polish and Italian, he managed to find an old register. Whilst our hopes were temporarily raised that there might be a Cieka birth recorded, they were soon dashed as the record only went back to 1945. We were unsure even then whether they were just for the Catholic church on Elcka Street. This was not the one attended by the Ciekas and where Paul is certain that he attended Sunday school from the age of four to the beginning of the flight as a refugee. But was it attached to the church, we ask ourselves? Paul seems convinced!

The museum in Orzysz had indicated that on one of my early photographs, one of the buildings on the main street was a Lutheran Sunday school and as we know, when Paul was in the process of preparing to leave Denmark for the UK, his father had given permission for a 5 year temporary stay in the UK provided Paul was brought up in the Lutheran tradition.

Lutheranism is a major branch of Western Christianity that identifies with the teaching of Martin Luther, a 16th-century German reformer. Luther's efforts to reform the theology and practice of the church launched the Protestant Reformation. The reaction of the government and church authorities to the international spread of his writings, beginning with the 95 Theses, divided Western Christianity.

On Paul's application form to join the NCH orphanage both father's and mother's religion is given as Lutheran. I certainly have no information to argue in favour of Paul attending the Lutheran Sunday School but simply include the information for the sake of completeness and because I have an old photo which shows this building.

Once again, my friend from Germany, Dietrich Peylo, has been able to solve the mystery of Paul's schooling. To assist with the identification of the location of the kindergarten and the school we will need a plan/map of Arys which is shown below.

The map on the next page is an early map of Arys, but the specific one that have used to identify various buildings associated with Paul's early childhood, was the one provided by the museum. This appears on page 152 and I apologise if while reading this section, the reader has to constantly refer back to this map and to the legend which accompanies the map.

It appears that the kindergarten was actually not next to the church but is shown on the map as being within in the "Evangelisches Gemeindehaus" opposite Nr. 17.

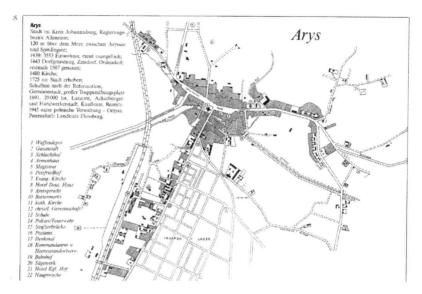

On the same map the position of the school is number 13. In the Dietrich Peylo Arys book, there is a picture of the school on page 57 taken about 1916. In 1936 it was renovated and received a second gable. I had thought that it was a pity that no picture postcard existed of the Arys-school between 1936 and 1945. But my good friend Dietrich has come up with the goods again as you will see. Amazingly, he has sent me a photograph of the staff as well. Brilliant! The attached coloured picture was taken in 2010. I think this school is now just an elementary school.

Relevant photographs of the school appear in the next few pages. But this is where the clarity of the details of the history of the school seems to be a bit in doubt. The modern picture is of the same school building that we saw on our visit in May 2019. But these buildings seem to date from just after the war. Indeed inside the building on the left side of the photograph there is a framed print hanging on the wall at the bottom of the staircase which provides a list of the first children in the school and which states from 1947. We did try to talk to a couple of adults and some children who were present but the language difficulty presented an insurmountable barrier.

Undeterred, we tried our luck at a second building across the square between the two buildings and managed to locate a school office. After some initial reticence, a lady, who appeared to be the school secretary, was able to summon another lady who appeared to be the director of the school who spoke excellent English.

We explained that we were trying to find out if these buildings had been in existence during World War II but it appeared that this present school dated from 1947 and the previous use, she claimed, was as a hospital. I'm not sure whether this conflicted with or confirmed the view of Katarzyna at the museum, who had previously indicated that when she investigated the history of the school she was told that no records existed prior to 1947. So we were left wondering was Paul's school on this site, was it the same building as that of the 1916 school but extensively renovated and modernised?

Paul was eight years old, when he left Arys and remembers attending church services and the kindergarten which apparently was near the school. But according to his age group he should have been at least in the second or even third school class. There were a number of classes and until 1945, the principal teachers were Paul Lelewel and Dr. Otto Nossag. We might be able to confirm this via Paul if he was able to remember the name of his male or female teacher?

Our walking tour then took us down the road to Elcka which also had a few old buildings, some much altered with modern uses but one apparently in the 1930s the house of a dentist and, apart from the satellite dishes, appears to retain its very traditional appearance. It has come as no surprise to me that many of the 1930s/1940s building have gone but one surprise was the existence of a very American looking diner but then again I remembered that I had read that there were a number of US troops stationed on the Orzysz base and even some Brits though I didn't notice any Roast Beef and Yorkshire Pudding on the menu! Apparently, I had read that the presence of such troops is due to some perceived/possible threat from Russian troops doing war games near the Polish border. Perhaps not much has changed sinc 1944.

Back on the road to Pisz, we came across a building which appeared, though altered, to be the former Kommandant's house, though not now on the camp as it is possible to walk to the main door. This is now a Cultural Centre and a person in authority, who gave us a guided tour, was able to confirm our suspicions about this building. Please see the photographs earlier in this chapter.

Although now not part of the camp, this magnificent edifice with its original staircase and doors plus a very traditional ceramic boiler must have been a magnificent property in its heyday. It had to be photographed and compared with the building on my old photograph which Paul has already recognised as the residence of the commander of the camp and I'm sure he will still identify it from my 2019 photograph. This was really brilliant and I had high hopes that perhaps the camp's press officer might come up with some modern photographs of some other old buildings still within the boundary of the camp.

von links nach rechts

1 Figura   Gutzeit 11
  2 Elxnat   Lellewel 10
    3 Worbs   Heinrich 9
      4 Wallhauer   Gottuk 8
        5 Sallet   Dr. Nossag 7
          6 Teichmüller

Arys school members of staff and the school below on the next page.

On thi spage is the school attended by Paul renovated and extended in 1936 with the photo on the previous page of the staff with their names, according to Dietrich Peylo

A German contact, Dietrich Peylo, born in1942, the last of 4 boys, given to me by the museum, who was able to help me with the history of Arys. He has confirmed that a number of people, unlike Paul and his mum, actually left Arys, in the face of the Russian advance west, by train. Indeed some members of his family left on the last train on 21 January 1945; the Russian offensive on Arys having begun on the 13th of January, although it appears that they didn't take control of the town until after the last train had departed Dietrich was convinced that the Ciekas wouldn't have left Arys until January 1945 as the German authorities, in the form of the Gauleiter, didn't give permission to leave the town until after the time Paul claims that he and his mum left i.e. in December 1944. Incidentally, the Peylos on their escape had an encounter with a Russian tank!

To my mind, it seems as once the residents of Arys, whether living on the camp or in the town, heard that the Russians were coming and fearing for their lives, would want to make their escape as quickly as possible rather than waiting for any bombardment on the town and the camp to begin. I would, wouldn't you?

The picture on page 108 is a map of Arys which Paul would recognise although I am not sure of its date. After the map is a key, translated by me from the original German, which I hope is reasonably accurate as I have relied on G translate.

It helps to understand the old postcards and it is a useful exercise to compare it with the modern map of Orzysz to see what has changed. The old map was also a great help to me in understanding what Paul had told me about Arys in our weekly chats in the past.

Below the reader will find a list of the numbers which appear on the map.

11-station, 12-cinema, Hindenburg Halle, 13 – officers restaurant/mess hall

14-soldiers accommodation, 15 – horse stables, 16 – house for soldiers

17 – cafe and kitchen, 18 – Station Street, 19 – hotel ' Koniglischer Hof'

20 – the photographer, 21 – Butcher, 22 – greenhouses, 23 – family residence

24 – Commandant's accommodation, 25 – site manager's office

26 – shared garden, 27 – military residents, 28 – Street, 29 – post office

30 – watch maker, 31 – shop selling coffee, confectionery, sweets

32 – tobacconists, 33 – church kindergarten (the one attended by Paul)

34 – new school, 35 – the old school (apparently according to my contact Dietrich Peylo, this school was burned down after the war due to welding works getting out of hand)

36 – men's and ladies hairdresser, 37 – butcher, 38 – shop selling toys and household utensils.

39 – canal/river, 40 – clothing shop, 41 – Paul's Church, 42 – soldiers accommodation

43 – Commandant's villa (see photographs), 44 – war memorial, 45 restaurant

More of the legend appears below the map on the next page.

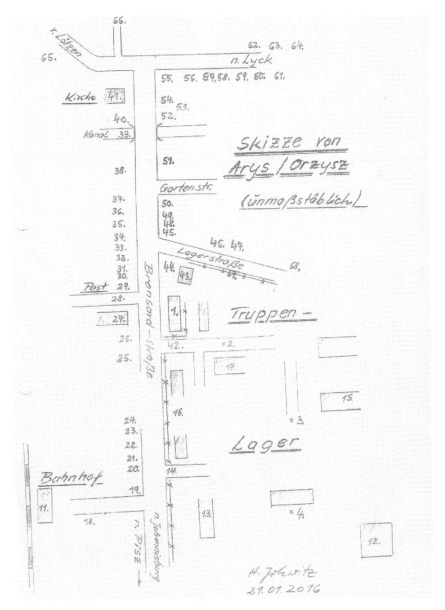

Skizze von Arys / Orzysz
(unmaßstäblich)

H. Jokwitz
27. 01. 2016

46 – cinema, 47 – dairy, 48 – bakery, 49 – shop selling toys, stationery, books, household items, giftware, 50 – doctors, 51 – shop selling food, drinks, building materials, heating material, hardware, 52 – bike shop (*coul this be the Weinke bike shop that Paul's mum took her bike to be repaired?*

53 and 54 – residences, 55 – Kaiser's coffee shop selling food and drinks and confectionery

56 butchers, 57 – German style restaurant which survived the war and dance hall

58 – residence, 59 – court building, 60 – residential building and pharmacy,

61 – Buttermarket *(one of the buildings remembered by Paul)*, 62 – Catholic Church

63 – shop selling stoves, 64 – bridge over the river, 65 – slaughterhouse, 66 Street

67 – residence, 68 – Hospital for soldiers

This map and its key was produced by Gruss Hubert in 2016.

This is a photograph of part of the current school which we saw on our visit which strangely looks very similar to the 1936 school.

Gruss aus ARYS. Neue Schule

The black and white photo above is of the old school, called 'new school, burnt down post WW2, which must have been Paul's school. Perhaps it was burnt down before the war as the one renovated and extended in 1936 look more like the modern version. Who knows, it's a mystery!. Perhaps a future reader of this book will be able to explain the chronology of the school.

The Arys railway station as it appeared in 2019.

Sadly, this building is now unused and has seen better days although it must have been a very attractive building its heyday. I was keen to visit and photograph it as Paul, as a young child, took trips on the railway and often went to visit the trains with his uncle so I was sure that he would remember it. Katarzyna at the museum has confirmed by email back in the UK that as far as she can remember the last time a train was at the station was about 20 years ago. Apparently, in February this year there was an event where people could travel by train to Ełk to. It was a nostalgic trip and a reminder of railway times.

The picture above which is the same view as my 2019 photo overleaf, dates from1941 so is the building as Paul would have seen it, whilst the view on the next page is the platform side which I am sure would also had been very familiar to Paul.

Anyway, on our visit, before we actually left the town, there were two other buildings I wanted to investigate. One was the existing hospital on K.Cierniaka. But it is not on the old plan of Arys and so it must be a more recent addition. The other was the large imposing building on the west side of the road to Pisz with the date 1906 on its pediment at its front elevation. Unfortunately, I haven't been able to find out much about this building, although it could have been the Hotel Koniglicher Hof.

Bahnhof Arys

Our visit completed, we headed back to Pisz to our accommodation, hopeful of spotting the site of the local airfield at Roski but decided to leave this bit of site investigation until the next day.

We were fortunate enough to find the airfield, on the next day, on our way to visit the Wolfsschanze, the Wolf's Lair, Hitler's military headquarters in World War II. The complex, which became one of several Führerhauptquartiere (Führer Headquarters) in various parts of Eastern Europe, was built for the start of Operation Barbarossa – the invasion of the Soviet Union – in 1941. It was constructed by Organisation Todt using 2-3 thousand workers from 1940-41.

Organisation Todt (OT) was a civil and military engineering organisation in Nazi Germany from 1933 to 1945, named for its founder, Fritz Todt, an engineer and senior Nazi. The organization was responsible for a huge range of engineering projects both in Nazi Germany and in occupied territories from France to the Soviet Union during World War II. It became notorious for using forced labour. From 1943-45 during the late phase of the Third Reich, OT administered all constructions of concentration camps to supply forced labour to industry.

The top secret, high security site was in the Masurian woods about 8 km (5.0 mi) east of the small East Prussian town of Rastenburg (now in Gierłoż, Kętrzyn County, Poland). Three security zones surrounded the central complex where the Führer's bunker was located. These were guarded by personnel from the SS Reichssicherheitsdienst and the Wehrmacht's armoured Führerbegleitbrigade. Despite the security, the most notable assassination attempt was by Claus Von Stauffenberg and others to assassinate Adolf Hitler and remove the Nazi Party from power. It was made at the Wolf's Lair on 20 July 1944. *But this is a story for another time.*

Our visit to the Roski airfield was very low key although we were surprised at the scale and nature and construction of the airfield access road from the main road, in that it appeared to be quite inappropriate for its current low-level use. This was surely evidence of the importance attached to the airfield in the past.

Our arrival seemed to cause a bit of a stir among the half-dozen or so men pottering about and tinkering with two PZL-Mielec M-18 Dromader aircraft. This light aeroplane is a single engine agricultural aircraft manufactured in Poland and is used mainly as a crop duster or firefighting/fire protection machine. This was confirmed by the pilot who was not very keen to talk to us probably wondering who we were. Well you would, wouldn't you, two strangers turning up out of the blue who were clearly not local and who couldn't speak a word of Polish.

However as luck would have it there was a friendlier Pole, who was keen to chat to us in perfect English. But first he asked us to move our car behind the only building on site, a prefabricated double garage because the whole area including the airfield was still under military control. It was the military who gave permission for the aircraft to do the crop spraying and fire protection duties. Naturally we obliged but later had it confirmed that the existing grass runway would have been a grass runway in the Second World War. He was keen to respond to our statement that a friend of ours, as a child and previous resident of the army base, had with other children from the local school in Rays, waved flags as Adolf Hitler arrived to inspect prototype Tiger tanks. He confirmed however, that indeed Adolf Hitler had visited the airfield and the army base, not once but four times! Amazing! Photographs were taken o the grass runway. However, this airfield had another story to tell and one which was quite different to that we had been told by that group of Poles we met in May 2019 as described below.

Roski airfield has many names including in Polish: Lotnisko Rostki, but it is also known as Lotnisko Orzysz Rostki and in German: Flugplatz Rotstken, or Flugplatz Arys-Rostken.

The decision to build the airfield in this location was apparently taken in 1936. For the local population, to hide the real reason that the airfield was being built, presumably for military purposes, the story was that it was for the Johannisburg Aeroclub. So the decision did not run into any opposition from the local community. The region was very poor, and the price for the land was good plus also many locals found employment in the construction of the airfield which lasted until 1938.

Concrete runways were in fact built, 2 kilometres long and 20 metres wide, masked to look like access roads to the nearby village. This is exactly the same roads that we had driven along on our way to the airfield. I did think that the roads were a bit over the top. A taxiing track was built under camouflage nets in the forest and airfield buildings were constructed in the forest and in the village. The conning tower was built between the tall pine trees on the hillside and the local cemetery. I'm not sure where these where, in any case we didn't see them.

In 1939, the villagers of Rostki saw Stukas and Jagdgeschwader 21 Me109Ds taking off for deployment in the Poland campaign. The scenes were repeated in 1941 during Operation Barbarossa, the invasion of Russia. But it seems for the most part that it was otherwise, used mainly as a practic field for trainers.

Between 15 and 20 September, year unknown, the airfield was the scene of remarkable event. Luftwaffe officers were dressed at their best and the local expected another visit by Hermann Göring. He frequently visited the airfiel and the region to go hunting, staying at the Göring-Quarters in Breitenheide in Polish: Szeroki Bór Piski. This time he was accompanied by Adolf Hitler who he had invited on a hunting trip so as to celebrate the fact that they had rescued Mussolini. The Italians had just surrendered to the Allies. Local witnesses reported Hitler looked very pleased. It is not known whether this is the same time that Paul and the other children were present to wave their flags on Hitler's arrival.

In 1944 the combat units returned to the airfield. Many returned damaged from their missions, until the Soviets occupied the area around the end of 1944. Unfortunately no pre-1990 photos have been located to indicate how the airfield may have looked in the past although it is probable that a few sheds and other buildings were available to be used for repairs and maintenance. An Internet search has revealed that the Jagdgeschwader 1.which was a fighter wing of the air force of the Luftwaffe, within eastern Prussia was deployed to the Arys-Rostken airfield.

After the war the airfield buildings were blown up with only the concrete foundations and the concrete taxi track still left remaining. The entire area was turned into a military training area with an exercise grass airfield. During the exercises the airfield would be mostly used by helicopters and it was abandoned after the fall of the Warsaw Pact which ceased to exist on July 1st, 1991.

Parts of the ring road were covered with asphalt until about 1996. Most of the rest of the airfield was destroyed by the war and later the Soviets. On 23rd January 1945: the town of Arys and the local airfield were taken by Soviet forces. Stories still circulate in the village about the existence of underground fuel tanks still holding aviation fuel although the Luftwaffe was notoriously short on fuel in the final year. Villagers also claim that the area is still hiding supplies of weapons and even a motor boat that was used for guerrilla-like tactics against the Soviets.

Although it is no longer an official airfield, it is, however, still used as a landing site for military exercises. Polish sources on the internet suggest the concrete runway may still be at the airfield, but overgrown with grass.

This is a relatively recent shot of the runway which is still used by aircraft on crop spraying and fire protection duties.

For more detailed information on the units that served on the airfield please refer to 'Luftwaffe Airfields 1939-45 (1937 Borders)' by Henr L. de Zeng IV who together the web site 'Abandoned Forgotten and Little Known Airfields in Europe' have provided valuable information for this book including photographs, for which I am eternally grateful.

With our visit to Orzysz now over, we journeyed to other parts of Poland and then returned to the UK. I was still hopeful that some of th contacts that were made during our short stay in the town would provide more information. As it turned out I was not to be disappointed.

Above is a photo of believed to be a former taxi way with the source photosik of Poland.

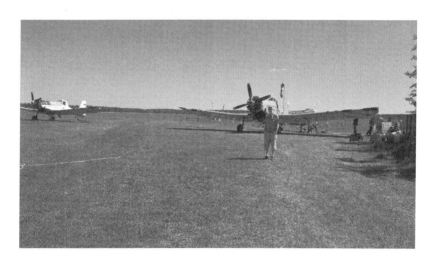

This photograph is the same as the one on the rear cover and is of the author at the Roski airfield taken in May 2019.

Chapter 10
Postscript to Visit to Poland

On returning to home, I was very pleased to find that Katarzyna, at the museum in Orzysz continued to be very helpful, providing information on different old buildings that I had identified on my trip to the town which Pau might remember from the 1930s and 1940s. Also, I was able to include some text from the exhibitions in the museum concerning the history of Arys which I'm pleased to say had actually been in English!

My German contact, provided by Katarzyna, Dietrich Peylo, bless him, following my emails to him had done his own detective work and found Paul's brother's name in the German telephone directory. Very quickly he had made contact and had spoken to him about the family Cieka. He also managed to find the family in the "Seelenliste" (list of souls?) assembled in about 1955 as follows:

Cika,	Paul	(1908)	*Note the different spelling*
Wehrmachts Beamter - military official			
Cika,	Lydia, geb.Schröder	(1910)	Frau
Cika,	Paul Robert	(1936)	Sohn
Cika,	Hans-Peter	(1946)	Sohn

This it would appear, is a significant document, comprising about a hundred and 50 pages, initiated by the B M V F K which appears to be the German minister for the expelled, for refugees and for war victims. He organised a fund for expropriation and eviction compensation.

Apparently, there were no more details about the name Schröder, Paul's mum's maiden name and he couldn't find either Cieka nor Schröder in the telephone list or address-list of the Arys-fellowship, the 'Gemeinschaft Arys.'

This was amazing. This was my first documentary link with Paul's birthplace and the family's connection to Arys actually provided by a document in German and I actually had a copy of the relevant extract. Apparently, the former inhabitants of Arys have a get together every year, I doubt that Paul knows about this. Every year the number attending is less which is not surprising and at the last event there were 14.

My contact with Dietrich, such is the value of the Internet, has resulted in him providing a number of interesting titbits of information which are actually included in the main body of the text of this book under appropriate headings. It also has provided me with another link to the history of the military town of Arys in the 1930s and 1940s.

The writing of this book has been an amazing journey which has taken me to Copenhagen, Denmark and Orzysz, Poland, to Paul's birthplace, to the Danish National Archives and Immigration Museum at Farum. It has given me an insight into life in 1930s and 1940s East Prussia and also what it was like to live in Danish refugee camps, as a German civilian, after the Second World War. It was also taken me to the headquarters of Action for Children, the successor to the National Children's Home where I examined the file which gave me an insight into the reason that the NC H and the UK Home Office decided to rescue German children from the poor, unsanitary and deprived conditions of the Danish refugee camps.

This journey has been an exciting and incredible look into the past of a dear friend and the experiences of the Ciekas. Yes, it has, at times, been frustrating due the bureaucracy of officialdom and the language barrier. But I wouldn't have missed any part of this fantastic journey for the world. It has revealed information which has been so surprising and my only hope is that you, the reader and others like you will find it an amazing read too.

Bibliography

From 'Arys to Harwich' draws on the many books, articles, exhibitions and web sites listed below:

Alrich, Amy A, '*Germans displaced from the* East*: Crossing Actual and Imagined Central European Borders, 1944-1955.*' 2003.
Blosmer, Jens, Refugee Administration, Letter to Gertrude Evans, World Council of Churches, 2nd December 1947.
Christensen, Peter A, '*A report on Horup Klint. 1: Annual Report for Loca, History Association for Horup*' (1986)

Compensation Cases, County of Aabenraa- Sonderburg, More Packages. In Landssarkivet for Sonderjylland.

Erstatningssager, Aabenraa-Sønderborg Amt. Flere pakker. I: Landsarkivet for Sønderjylland.

Neilson, Leif Hansen, e-mail regarding refugee camps in the Sonderburg area of Denmark, 23/08/2016.

(Lynne Fallwell, 'Modern German Midwifery, 1885–1960.')

Havrehed, Henrik 'The German refugees in Denmark 1945-1949.'

Ertel, Manfred, '*A Legacy of Dead German Children*', Spiegel Online, 16 May 2005.

Frau Lampracht and Frau Knoblauch letters about Grove camp in 1946 and 1947, published June 2 016.

Institut for Sønderjysk Lokalhistorie.

Lutterberg Charlotte – Remembers Horupklint

Marckmann, Anton (2006): *'The German submarines at the bottom o Horup Hav. In sonderjysk Yearbooks.'*

Merten, Ulrich *'Forgotten Voices, The Expulsion of the Germans from* Eastern *Europe After World War II'*, *Transaction Publishers London, 2013.*

Mix, Karl George, 'Deutsche Fluchtlinge in Danemark, 1945-1949.'

Oberg, Alfred TH, *'Danmark I Billeder.'* 1950.

Orzysz web site, Poland.

Peylo, Dietrich, 'Arys/Ostpreussen in Bilddokumenten. 2009.

Statens Civile Luftvaerns.

Appendix 1

The Cieka Family Tree i)

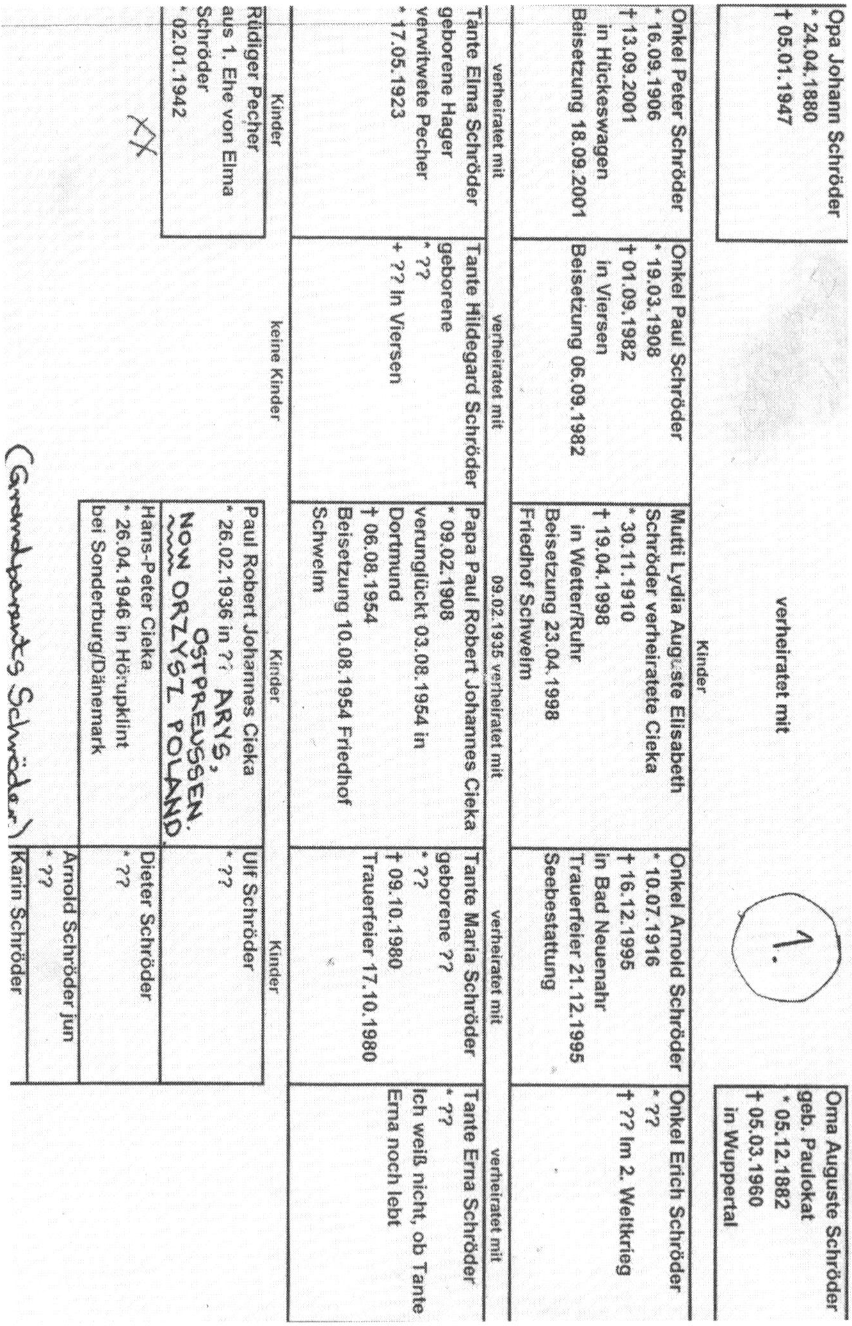

Opa Johann Schröder				
* 24.04.1880				
† 05.01.1947				

verheiratet mit

Oma Auguste Schröder
geb. Paulokat
* 05.12.1882
† 05.03.1960
in Wuppertal

(circled) 1.

Kinder

Onkel Peter Schröder	Onkel Paul Schröder	Mutti Lydia Auguste Elisabeth Schröder verheiratete Cieka	Onkel Arnold Schröder	Onkel Erich Schröder
* 16.09.1906	* 19.03.1908	* 30.11.1910	* 10.07.1916	* ??
† 13.09.2001	† 01.09.1982	† 19.04.1998	† 16.12.1995	† ?? Im 2. Weltkrieg
in Hückeswagen	in Viersen	in Wetter/Ruhr	in Bad Neuenahr	
Beisetzung 18.09.2001	Beisetzung 06.09.1982	Beisetzung 23.04.1998 Friedhof Schwelm	Trauerfeier 21.12.1995 Seebestattung	

verheiratet mit	verheiratet mit	09.02.1935 verheiratet mit	verheiratet mit	verheiratet mit
Tante Elma Schröder geborene Hager verwitwete Pecher	Tante Hildegard Schröder geborene	Papa Paul Robert Johannes Cieka	Tante Maria Schröder geborene ??	Tante Erna Schröder
* 17.05.1923	* ??	* 09.02.1908	* ??	* ??
	† ?? in Viersen	verunglückt 03.08.1954 in Dortmund	† 09.10.1980	Ich weiß nicht, ob Tante Erna noch lebt
		† 06.08.1954	Trauerfeier 17.10.1980	
		Beisetzung 10.08.1954 Friedhof Schwelm		

Kinder	keine Kinder	Kinder	Kinder	
Rüdiger Pecher aus 1. Ehe von Elma Schröder		Paul Robert Johannes Cieka	Ulf Schröder	
* 02.01.1942		* 26.02.1936 in ?? ARYS, *OSTPREUSSEN.* NOW ORZYSZ, POLAND.	* ??	
		Hans-Peter Cieka	Dieter Schröder	
		* 26.04.1946 in Hörupklint bei Sonderburg/Dänemark	* ??	
			Arnold Schröder jun	
			* ??	
			Karin Schröder	

(handwritten) (Grandparents Schröder)

(handwritten marking: ✗✗)

166

The Cieka Family Tree ii)

Tante Gertrud Cieka
verheiratete Neumann
* 18.06.1897
† 06.10.1974

verheiratet mit

Alfred Neumann
* ??
† 1960 in Rendsburg
beigesetzt in Rendsburg

keine Kinder

Kinder

Tante Elisabeth Cieka
* 04.10.1905
† 01.10.1973
in Rendsburg
Urnenbeisetzung
16.10.1973 in
Rendsburg

nicht verheiratet

Papa Paul Robert Johannes Cieka
* 09.02.1908
verunglückt 03.08.1954 in Dortmund
† 06.08.1954
Beisetzung 10.08.1954 Friedhof
Schwelm

Zwillinge
Es sollen noch
Zwillinge geboren
worden sein, die bei
der Geburt verstorben
sind. Nähere Angaben
habe ich nicht

verheiratet mit

Mutti Lydia Auguste Elisabeth Cieka
geborene Schröder
* 30.11.1910
† 19.04.1998
in Wetter/Ruhr
Beisetzung 23.04.1998
Friedhof Schwelm

Kinder

Paul Robert Johannes Cieka
* 26.02.1936 in ?? ORZYSZ.
Hans-Peter Cieka
* 26.04.1946 in Hörupklint
bei Sonderburg/Dänemark

The Cieka Family Tree iii)

Oma Elise Cieka
geb. Richnau
* 25.07.1874
† etwa 21.09.1945

Appendix 2

German Refugees in Danish Refugee Camps-Numbers

The number of German refugees between 1945 and 1949

05/08/1945:   244,493

01/07/1946:   198, 001

01/07/1947:   123, 906

01/07/1948:   44, 785

01/01/1949:   2,365

Source: 'State Civil Air Defence and Refugees Administration's National Register.

Distribution by age and gender (15/08/1946)

Age	Men	Women	Total
0-14	34,580	32, 978	67, 558
15 – 19	7, 843	11, 892	19, 735
20 – 34	2, 016	29, 905	31, 921
35 – 54	8, 182	36, 901	45, 083
55 – 74	11, 440	17, 503	8, 943
75+	1, 343	1, 935	3,278
Total	65, 404	131, 114	196, 518

Source: Medical Statistics for 1946.

Appendix 3
Places that Paul and Lydia Cieka
Intended to Visit or Actually Visited
On Their Journey from Arys to Denmark

Lotzen (Gizycko)

Osterode

Preushiss Holland (Paslek)

Ebling (Eblag)

Frisches Haff

Konigsberg (Kaliningrad)

Wormditt (Orneta)

Danzig (Gdansk)

Strahlsrund

Sellin (Isle of Ruggen)

Flensborg

Appendix 4

Danish Refugee Registration Cards

Lejrkort for tyske Flygtninge i Danmark

Lejradresse — Lageradresse

Datum	Lejrnr.	Lejradresse

1. Gricka — Efternavn — Familienname
2. Schroeder — Pigenavn — Mädchenname
3. Lydia — Fornavne — Vornamen
4. Ehefrau — Livsstilling eller Uddannelse — Beruf oder Ausbildung
5. verh. — Stilling i Familien — Familienstand
6. evgl. — Religion

Kortet medfølger ved Flytning. Flytning not. i ovenst. Rubrik. Die Karte geht bei Verlegung mit. Verlegungen in obiger Rubrik vermerken. — Registr. Nummer

7. 30.11.40 — født den — geb. am, (Datum und Jahr)

8. Fødested — Geburtsort (Stadt oder Dorf, Kreis, Provinz)
9. sidste faste Adresse — letzte feste Anschrift (Stadt oder Dorf, Kreis, Provinz, Postnummer)
10. sidste Adr. i Tyskland — letzte Anschrift in Deutschland (Stadt oder Dorf, Kreis, Provinz, Postnummer)

Lejrkort for tyske Flygtninge i Danmark

Lejradresse — Lageradresse

Datum	Lejrnr.	Lejradresse

1. Gricka — Efternavn — Familienname
2. Pigenavn — Mädchenname
3. Hans-Peter — Fornavne — Vornamen
4. Kind — Livsstilling eller Uddannelse — Beruf oder Ausbildung
5. led. — Stilling i Familien — Familienstand
6. evgl. — Religion

Kortet medfølger ved Flytning. Flytning not. i ovenst. Rubrik. Die Karte geht bei Verlegung mit. Verlegungen in obiger Rubrik vermerken. — Registr. Nummer

7. 26.4.46 — født den — geb. am, (Datum und Jahr)

8. Fødested — Geburtsort (Stadt oder Dorf, Kreis, Provinz)
9. sidste faste Adresse — letzte feste Anschrift (Stadt oder Dorf, Kreis, Provinz, Postnummer)
10. sidste Adr. i Tyskland — letzte Anschrift in Deutschland (Stadt oder Dorf, Kreis, Provinz, Postnummer)

Printed in Great Britain
by Amazon